Chapter 1
A Green Majority

Our political thinking has not caught up with the unprecedented change that occurred in America during the twentieth century, the change from a scarcity economy to a surplus economy.

In the year 1900, the average American's income was near what we now define as the poverty level. Large-scale industry was expanding production dramatically, and there was widespread hope that economic growth could relieve poverty. Socialists – joined later in the century by New Deal and Great Society liberals – wanted the government to make sure that economic growth would benefit working people.

In the year 2000, the average American's income was more than five times what it had been a century earlier. During the twentieth century, America was the first society in history to move from scarcity to wide-spread affluence. Yet liberals kept focusing on the same policies that they supported to alleviate poverty early in the century: the government should spend money to provide more health care, provide more education, provide more housing, and provide other services.

Liberals kept focusing on the problems of scarcity. We still have not caught up with the fact that, for most Americans, the age-old problem of scarcity has become less important than the new problems caused by affluence – problems such as traffic congestion, urban sprawl, shortages of natural resources, and global warming.

Most important, liberals have not realized that supporting the consumerist standard of living is a huge burden for most Americans, leaving us without enough time for our families and for our own interests. They have not realized that most of us would be better off if we could downshift economically and have more free time rather than consuming more.

Environmentalists focus on the problems caused by economic growth, but they have not come up with a positive vision of the future that would help relieve these environmental problems and would also give us a more satisfying way of life than we have in today's consumer society.

We need to replace the old politics of scarcity with a new politics of simple living, with policies such as:

- **Work-Time Choice:** Today, most people have no choice but to take full-time jobs, because most part-time jobs have lower hourly pay and no benefits. We need policies that make it possible to choose part-time work, so people have the option of working shorter hours, consuming less, and having more free time.

- **Neighborhood Choice:** Since World War II, federal freeway policies and local zoning laws have forced most American cities to be rebuilt as low-density sprawl where people cannot leave their houses without driving. We need to build walkable, transit-oriented neighborhoods, so people have the option of reducing the huge economic burden of automobile dependency.

- **Child-Care Choice:** Today, we subsidize families who use day care, but we do nothing to help families who work shorter hours to care for their own children. We should give families with preschool children a tax credit that they could use to pay for day care or could use to work shorter hours and have more time to care for their own children.

Policies like these would appeal to the majority of Americans because they address the key failing of the modern economy – the fact that increasing consumerism and economic growth no longer provide increasing human satisfaction. If Americans had these choices, many people would decide they would be happier if they consumed less and had more time for themselves and their families. Today, most people do not even have the option of living simpler and more satisfying lives.

Policies like these are essential to preserving the global environment. Endless economic growth is causing global warming, depletion of energy resources, and potential ecological collapse. Other policies are also needed to protect the environment, such as shifting from fossil fuels to renewable energy, but these technological fixes are not enough by themselves. We must ultimately adopt policies that move us beyond our hypergrowth economy. The only question is how much damage we will do to the global environment before we address this issue.

Policies like these provide us with a vision of a better future. In the early twentieth century, liberals appealed to most Americans by promising a future where economic growth brought affluence to everyone. But in America, we have reached a point where this vision of increasing affluence is no longer compelling because most Americans already have enough. A world with even more freeways and even bigger SUVs for everyone is not an inspiring vision of the future – even apart from global warming and energy shortages. Instead of endless growth and consumerism, we need a vision of a future where everyone has enough income to live a comfortable middle-class life, and where everyone has enough free time to live well.

Why isn't this politics of simple living part of today's political debate? Liberals should not stop advocating policies that help the minority of Americans who are poor, but we should focus on advocating policies that let the affluent majority decide when they have enough. We should focus on policies that let middle-class Americans choose whether they want to consume more or whether they want to have more time for their families, their communities, and their own interests.

Not all Americans are such frantic consumers as they sometimes seem to be. The problem is that they do not have the choice of downshifting economically, because of the jobs available to them, because of the way we build our cities, and because of the way we package social services such as child care. Our society is designed to promote consumerism.

When the Socialist Party advocated unemployment insurance and the 40 hour work week in 1900, these policies were denounced as radical, but within a few decades, Americans took these policies for granted. Something similar could happen if environmentalists begin to advocate policies that give people the choice of living simpler and more satisfying lives. Within a few decades, we could have a green majority.

Chapter 2
Downshifting and Work-Time Choice

There is a question that is critical to determining what sort of lives we live and whether our economy is environmentally sustainable, but that no mainstream American politician has talked about for seven decades. That question is: Should we take advantage of our increasing productivity to consume more or to have more free time?

Ever since the beginning of the industrial revolution, improved technology has allowed the average worker to produce more in an hour of work. During the twentieth century, productivity (the term that economists use for output per worker hour) grew by an average of about 2.3 percent a year – which means that the average American worker in 2000 produced about eight times as much in one hour as the average worker in 1900.

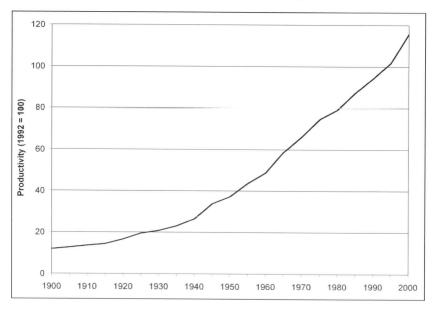

Figure 1: American Productivity (Output per Worker Hour)[2]

During the nineteenth and early twentieth century, workers took advantage of higher productivity and higher wages both to earn more income and to work shorter hours: average earnings rose and the average work week declined consistently. Workers had more to consume and had more free time.

But in post-war America, the trend toward shorter hours suddenly stopped. Since 1945, in a dramatic break with the historical trend, we have used the entire gain in productivity to produce and consume more, and we have not increased the average worker's free time at all. In fact, we have done something even more extreme than that; during the past several decades, work hours have gotten longer, and we actually work more now than we did in 1975.

We could reduce global warming and many other environmental problems by taking a more balanced approach: instead of using higher productivity just to increase consumption, we could also use it to reduce work hours, as we did during most of our history.

Losing the Fight over Work Time

If we look at the history of the struggle between labor and management over work hours, we can see that Americans today do not work long hours out of free choice, as conservative economists claim. Though most people do not remember it today, there was a political struggle over work hours during the 1930s that led to the deliberate political decision to set a standard work week of 40 hours and to stimulate economic growth rapid enough to provide workers with these 40-hour jobs.

During the nineteenth and early twentieth century, unions fought for shorter hours just as fiercely as they fought for higher wages. Because of these struggles, the average work week in manufacturing declined dramatically, from about 70 hours in 1840 to 40 hours a century later.

In the early nineteenth century, the typical American factory worker earned subsistence wages by working six days a week, twelve hours a day. For example, in Lowell, Massachusetts, factories were established as part of a humanitarian social experiment meant to give young women a place to work and to save a bit of money before marriage; and even these humanitarian reformers required women to work 12 hours a day, six days a week, with only four holidays per year apart from Sundays.

In England, wages were lower than in America, so factory workers had to toil for even longer hours to earn subsistence, and children had to work as well as adults. In 1812, one manufacturer in Leeds, England, was described as humane because he did not allow children to work more than 16 hours a day.[3]

Gradually, as new technology allowed workers to produce more per hour, wages went up, and the work week declined. As Figure 2 shows, the work week in manufacturing (where we have the best statistics) declined steadily through the nineteenth century and early twentieth century. During the 1920s, Americans moved from the traditional six-day week to a five-and-a-half-day work week, with half of Saturday off as well as Sunday. During the 1930s, we adopted the five-day, 40-hour week.

In the early twentieth century, unions continued to fight for shorter hours as well as for higher wages. For example, William Green, president of the American Federation of Labor, wrote in 1926 that "The human values of leisure are even greater than its economic significance," because leisure is needed "for the higher development of spiritual and intellectual powers."[5]

During the 1930s, the great depression gave labor unions another reason to fight for shorter hours: a shorter work week would reduce unemployment by sharing the available work. The Black-Connery bill, passed by the Senate on April 6, 1933, would have made the work week 30 hours to reduce unemployment. When this bill was introduced in congress, labor supported it strongly, with William Green as a leader.

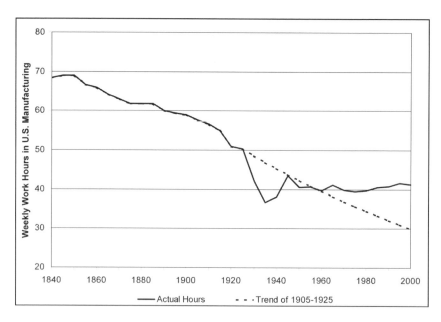

Figure 2: Average Work Week in US Manufacturing[4]

At the time, most people believed that the 30-hour week would just be the first step. The depression seemed to be caused by inadequate demand: most people were beginning to reach the point where they had enough to be comfortable economically and did not need to consume much more. As technology continued to improve and workers continued to produce more each hour, it seemed inevitable that workers would produce everything that people wanted in fewer and fewer work hours, so the work week would have to keep getting shorter to avoid unemployment.

But business leaders opposed the Black-Connery bill fiercely, and they said that instead of shortening hours, we should fight unemployment by promoting what they called "a new gospel of consumption." Initially, the Roosevelt administration had backed Black-Connery, but because of business opposition, it abandoned its support for this bill and instead worked for a compromise that would satisfy both business and labor. Without Roosevelt's support, Black-Connery failed by just a few votes in the House of Representatives.

Roosevelt's compromise plan had two features: the 40-hour week, and government programs to stimulate the economy and provide jobs.

The Fair Labor Standards Act of 1938 set the standard work week at 40 hours, which did not actually reduce work hours for most workers, since average work hours had already declined to less than that because of the depression.

In addition to setting this standard work week, the Roosevelt administration made every effort to stimulate the economy through federal spending, in order to give each worker one of those 40-hour jobs. For example, under Roosevelt's New Deal, the federal government built highways, dams, and other public works to stimulate the economy.

After World War II, Roosevelt's compromise – the forty-hour week plus policies to stimulate the economy and provide more forty-hour jobs – became the status quo. We still live with this compromise today.

In post-war America, there were fears that the economy would fall back into depression. The federal government dealt with the potential problem of inadequate consumer demand by spending vast sums of money to stimulate the economy. For example, there were federal programs to build freeways and to guarantee mortgages for new suburban housing, and there was bipartisan support for Keynesian economics and federal deficit spending to encourage rapid economic growth.

The private sector also did its share by spending more on advertising, and our leaders told us that it was our obligation to listen to the advertising and buy the products. In one famous example, a reporter asked President

Eisenhower what Americans could do to help end the recession of 1958, and this dialog followed:

Eisenhower: Buy.
Reporter: Buy what?
Eisenhower: Anything.[6]

These efforts succeeded in stimulating growth that was rapid enough to give Americans those standard 40-hour jobs. In a reversal of the historical trend, the work-week did not decline during the 1950s and 1960s, despite widespread economic prosperity and higher wages.

Since the 1970s, the average work-week has actually increased, because more women have entered the workforce, and because employers have pressured full-time workers to work longer hours. Economist Juliet Schor estimates that the average American worker today works 160 hours per year longer than in the 1960s.[7]

Despite the tremendous changes in our society and the tremendous growth of our economy since the 1930s, Roosevelt's compromise is still with us today. Everyone accepts the idea that people should have standard 40-hour-a-week jobs, and every politician promises to stimulate the economy to provide more of these standard 40-hour jobs.

Our society is out of balance because we have spent more than a half century focusing on increased consumption and ignoring increased free time. Because women entered the workforce during that period, many families now face a time famine, without enough free time to take care of their own children. If today's time-starved Americans knew the history of the battle over work hours, most would probably feel that they would be better off if Black-Connery had passed and given us a 30-hour week.

Choice of Work Hours

Most Americans today have no choice of work hours. In general, the good jobs are full-time jobs. Most part-time jobs have low wages, no benefits, no seniority, and no opportunity for promotion.

You can get a part-time job if you want to work the cash register at a fast-food restaurant, but you usually have to take a full-time job if you want to work as a plumber, an engineer, an accountant, a lawyer, or if you want most any other job with security, benefits, and decent pay. To give a glaring example of our unfairness to part-time workers, many college teachers now work part time as "Adjunct Professors," and they are paid far less per course than full-time professors, they have no benefits, and they have no chance of being promoted and getting tenure.

Studies have shown that 85 percent of male workers have no choice of hours – their only choice is a full-time job or no job.[8] Economist Juliet Schor has estimated that, if the average male worker cuts his hours in half, he will cut his earnings by more than 80 percent because of the lower pay and benefits for part-time workers;[9] the average woman would lose less, but that is only because women are more likely to work part-time, so they already have lower wages because of discrimination against part-time workers.

A survey by the Center for the New American Dream found that half of American full-time workers would prefer to work four days a week at 80% of their current earnings – but they do not have this choice.[10]

Despite the low pay, many people choose to work part time. The great majority of part-time workers are part-time by choice, and only 17 percent work part time because full time work is not available.[11] Obviously, many more people would want to work part time, if part-time workers were treated as well as full-time workers.

To give people the choice of consuming less and having more free time, we should adopt policies that let people choose their work hours, as some European nations have already done:

- **End discrimination against part-time workers:** By law, employees who do the same work should get the same hourly pay, whether they are full-time or part-time. Part-time workers also should have the same seniority and same chance of promotion as full-time workers, with seniority based on the total number of hours an employee has worked. The entire European Union has already adopted policies like these to end discrimination against part-time workers.

- **Allow workers to choose part-time jobs:** The Netherlands and Germany have laws saying that, if a full-time employee asks to work shorter hours, the employer must accommodate the request unless it will be a hardship to the business; only 4% of these requests are rejected because of hardship. These laws are the ideal, but if they are too strong for us to adopt immediately, we can begin by giving private employers tax incentives or other incentives to provide high-quality part-time jobs and to let employees choose their work hours.

The Netherlands was the first country to adopt policies encouraging part-time work. During the 1980s, under the agreement of Wassenaar, labor unions moderated their wage demands in exchange for employers providing more part-time jobs; at the same time, the Netherlands passed a law forbidding discrimination against part-time workers, which has since been adopted by the entire European Union. More recently, the Netherlands has required employers to accommodate requests for shorter hours, if they do not cause economic hardship. As a result of all these policies, the Netherlands has almost as many part-time as full-time workers, and the average Dutch worker now works only about three-quarters as many hours as the average American worker.[12]

Rudd Lubbers, the Prime Minister when the agreement of Wassenaar was implemented, has written:

> The Dutch are not aiming to maximize gross national product per capita. Rather, we are seeking to attain a high quality of life.... Thus, while the Dutch economy is very efficient per working hour, the number of working hours per citizen is rather limited. ... We like it that way. Needless to say, there is more room for all those important aspects of our lives that are not part of our jobs, for which we are not paid and for which there is never enough time.[13]

These policies would not force anyone to work shorter hours, but they would give people the option of working shorter hours. They would let people choose whether they want to consume more or to have more free time.

Choice Versus Shorter Hours

In the past, work hours became shorter when the standard work week was reduced, but in today's society, there are reasons why it makes sense to let people choose their own hours rather than shortening the standard work week.

Choice of work hours accommodates recent changes in the family. Until a few decades ago, most families were supported by one male breadwinner. Today, families are much more diverse. Some people are the sole wage earners for their families, and they may need to work long hours to get by. Other families are made up of childless working couples who can easily afford to work shorter hours.

Choice of work hours has political advantages. It is hard politically to argue against choice: conservatives would argue against a shorter standard work week by saying that most people want to earn more and consume more, but it would be hard for them to argue against giving people a choice. In addition, a shorter standard work week creates conflicts between employers and employees because it raises costs for employers (which is why the 35-hour work week has become so controversial in France), but choice of work hours does not create this conflict (which is why this choice has not become controversial in Germany and the Netherlands).

Choice of work hours would reduce inequality of income, because people with higher hourly earnings are more likely to work shorter hours. Ultimately, it could change our definition of success: we would consider people successful if they not only have a higher income than average but also have more free time than average.

Most important, choice of work hours would allow people to make a deliberate choice of their standard of living. Each person would have to decide whether it is more important to consume more or to have more free time, and this choice would make people think much harder about their purchases. Instead of buying a McMansion and a Hummer, you could buy an average size house and a Toyota and work (say) one day less each week. If you have fixed work hours and a fixed salary, you might as well buy the biggest house and the biggest car you can afford; but if you have a choice of work hours, you have a reason to consume less.

Now that we have moved from a scarcity economy to a surplus economy, this choice of standard of living has become important economically.

In theory, choice of work hours has always made economic sense. Economic theory has always said that people should have a free choice among different products, so they can choose the one that gives them the most satisfaction. Economic theory implies that people should be able to choose between consuming more and having more free time for exactly the same reason – because they might get more satisfaction from increased free time than they get from increased consumption.

In practice, this choice was not very important in the past. In a scarcity economy, most people consumed not much more than the essentials, so they could not go very far in choosing more free time rather than more consumer goods. As a result, most economists overlooked the issue historically.

In our surplus economy, though, many people could get by with significantly less income and more free time than they now have. The choice between more free time and more income is now critical to determining what sort of lives people lead. We can no longer afford to overlook it.

This choice between more free time and more income is also important to dealing with our most pressing environmental problems. For example, a recent study by economist Mark Weisbrot found that, if Americans worked as few hours as western Europeans, it would lower our energy consumption and greenhouse gas emissions by 20 percent.[14]

A movement toward simpler living could help to reduce all our environmental problems. But that movement cannot become widespread until people are allowed to choose their work hours and to make a deliberate decision about whether they want to consume more or to have more free time.

Free Time for Free People

If they had the option, would people choose shorter hours? And what would they do with their extra free time?

There are some successful CEOs, architects, writers, musicians, and the like who would not reduce their hours, because they get more satisfaction from their work than they could get from any other activity. But people like these are relatively rare.

Even among people who get satisfaction from their jobs, most would be happier doing less of their routine work and spending more time on related activities that enrich their work. Most college professors would be happier with a lighter workload and more time for research and study. Most doctors and lawyers would be happier with a lighter workload and more time to keep up with developments in their fields.

The great majority of Americans – from accountants to computer programmers to electricians to middle managers – work primarily for income and not for the intrinsic satisfaction that they get from doing their jobs. If they did not need the money, they would gladly work less. If these people began to work shorter hours, many of them would use their free time to do work that pays little or nothing but that is satisfying in itself.

For example, Vince works as a policeman but devotes his weekends to his hobby of carving wooden doors. He began by carving a door for his own house, it looked so good that a few neighbors asked him to do the same for them, and soon he had so many people asking for his doors than he had trouble keeping up with demand. But he earns less than a dollar an hour carving doors, so it could never support him. He looks forward to retirement, so he can spend more time on this hobby.

Susan worked as an administrative assistant at a university. After her children were grown, she began volunteering with neighborhood groups and groups advocating affordable housing, and after a decade of volunteer work, she was elected to the city council. At that point, she essentially had two full-time jobs: as an administrative assistant during workdays, and as a councilmember virtually every evening and weekend – a pace that most people could not maintain. When she finally retired from the job where she earned her income, she still had more than a full-time workload as a councilmember.

Imagine how different our culture would be if Americans spent less time working to buy consumer goods and spent more time doing work that they love and are dedicated to. People could have creative second careers without quitting their day jobs, because their day jobs would not take as much time: they would have time to spend performing music, producing crafts, working in local community groups, being active in politics, and the like. Of course, they would also have more time to spend with their children, families, and friends. There could be an unprecedented flourishing of human talent.

Compulsory Consumption

For most Americans, though, choice of work hours is not enough in itself.

Upper-middle class Americans can cut their work hours significantly by giving up luxuries. We can see that there is plenty of wasteful spending to cut, just by looking at all the oversized SUVs on the roads, or by considering that the average new house built today is 65 percent larger than the average new house build in 1970,[15] or by considering that Americans spend three to four times as much time shopping as Europeans.[16]

But when we move beyond the upper-middle class and look at moderate-income Americans, we find that most people feel hard pressed economically. They will tell you that, if they cut their work hours by very much, they would not be able to get by.

When the Black-Connery bill was introduced during the 1930s, everyone thought it was plausible that that the typical wage earner could support a family working thirty hours a week. Today, Americans earn much more per hour than Americans did in the 1930s, but most Americans would be shocked by the idea that they could support their family with the income of one wage earner working a thirty-hour week.

The problem is that we are burdened with a large amount of compulsory consumption. In addition to allowing personal choice of work hours, we need larger social changes to give people the option of downshifting economically.

Chapter 3
Livable Cities and Neighborhood Choice

The way we build our cities and neighborhoods puts a tremendous economic burden on the average American.

Our spending on transportation has soared as our cities have been rebuilt around the automobile. One hundred years ago, most Americans who lived in cities and suburbs walked for most trips; if you did not commute to work, you spent nothing at all on transportation most days. Today, most Americans cannot leave their homes without driving, an economic burden that is getting worse as gasoline prices increase.

Our spending on suburban housing also involves a huge economic burden: the low-density, automobile-oriented suburban housing that most Americans live in today is much more expensive than the apartments, row houses, and streetcar suburbs that Americans lived in a century ago.

Most people do not have the choice of avoiding these costs. One hundred years ago, middle-class Americans lived in neighborhoods where they could walk on most trips. Today, zoning laws require most Americans to live in neighborhoods where they must drive to go anywhere at all.

Cities in the Consumer Society

This huge increase in spending on transportation and housing did not just happen. During the post-war period, government policies deliberately encouraged Americans to spend more on automobiles and suburban housing in order to stimulate the economy. This was part of the post-war consensus that grew out of Roosevelt's response to the depression: we needed economic growth rapid enough to provide everyone with a 40-hour-a-week job, and government promoted this growth by building public works, such as freeways, and by encouraging private investment, such as suburban development. The post-war economy considered the auto-dependent suburbs to be a key part of the "rising standard of living" that helped to absorb consumers' excess purchasing power and to create more 40-hour-a-week jobs.

But in retrospect, most city planners today agree that these policies caused the biggest problems of contemporary American cities: traffic congestion, less livable neighborhoods, destruction of open space, and high levels of energy consumption and greenhouse gas emissions.

The federal government began to promote automobile use during the 1930s, when the Roosevelt administration funded highways to provide construction jobs for the unemployed and to stimulate the economy by increasing demand for automobiles.

During the post-war period, the Eisenhower administration carried this approach much further by creating the 41,000 mile Interstate Highway System and by creating the Highway Trust Fund, which reserved revenues from gasoline taxes to be used only for highway spending, providing an endless source of funding for more highways. The Interstate System was touted as a defense project, but it was also meant to stimulate the economy: in fact, when this plan was adopted, Eisenhower's Secretary of Defense was Charles Wilson, previously chairman of General Motors, who was famous for saying "What's good for General Motors is good for the country"[17] Today, the Interstate Highway System dominates American transportation, with over 45,000 miles of roads.[18]

The federal government also began to promote suburbanization during the 1930s, to stimulate the economy. The Roosevelt administration built bedroom suburbs such as Greenbelt, Maryland. Even more important, it established the Federal Housing Authority in 1934 to insure home mortgages, and until the 1960s, the FHA offered financing only to new construction at suburban densities, helping to finance the huge boom of post-war suburban development.

During the post-war period, the federal policy of promoting suburbanization was astoundingly effective. In the single decade following 1950, for example, the number of dwelling units in the United States increased by 63 percent.[19] In just a few decades, freeway-oriented suburbs became the dominant form of community in America, largely as a result of federal freeway funding and FHA financing for suburban housing.

Yet all the money spent on freeways did not make transportation more convenient, and all the money spent on sprawl suburbs did not make neighborhoods more livable.

Freeways Mean More Traffic

Despite all the money spent on freeways, traffic kept getting worse. Early projections of traffic volumes on urban freeways always turned out to be underestimates, and freeways that were supposed to accommodate traffic for decades became congested within a year or two of being completed.

Today, city planners call this problem "induced demand." Building freeways allows people to travel faster, and so it encourages people to travel longer distances – to drive to regional shopping centers rather than to local shopping and to move to more remote suburbs and commute longer distances to work. Studies have shown that the time Americans spend traveling tends to remain roughly constant, and if transportation is faster, people travel longer distances.[20]

All the money we spend on freeways has not saved time or relieved traffic congestion. Instead, it has generated more traffic by encouraging people to drive longer distances. For example, one study found that, within five years after a major freeway is built in California, 95 percent of the new road capacity fills up with traffic that would not have existed if the road had not been built.[21] The distance that the average American drives has doubled since the 1960s.

Because of all the money we have spent on freeways, transportation is a major expense for most Americans, congestion is a constant problem, and getting around has become so nerve-racking that we have developed a new pathology called "road rage."

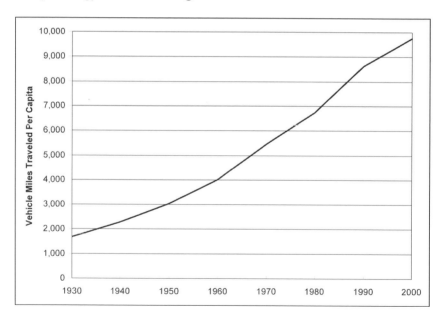

Figure 3. The distance an average American drives doubled since the 1960s.[22]

Sprawl Means Less Livability

Likewise, all the money we spend building lower density suburbs has not made neighborhoods more livable. We can see that lower densities have stopped making our cities more livable by looking at how middle-class American neighborhoods have changed over the last century.

One hundred years ago, the American middle class lived in streetcar suburbs,[23] which we think of today as the classic American neighborhood. They were made up of free-standing houses, with fairly large backyards, small front yards, and front porches looking out on tree-lined streets. Houses were commonly built on one-tenth acre lots.

These streetcar suburbs felt spacious and quiet compared with the city, but their most important form of transportation was still walking. Streetcars were used for commuting to work and for occasional trips to other parts of town, but everyone lived within walking distance of a neighborhood shopping street, where they could find the stores, doctors offices, and other services that they needed regularly, and where they could also find the streetcar stop that connected them with the rest of the city.

During the twentieth century, Americans moved to lower density suburbs. After World War I, typical middle-class neighborhoods were made up of bungalows on one-sixth acre lots: often, the neighborhood stores were not quite close enough to walk to easily, so people drove a few blocks to buy their groceries. After World War II, middle-class neighborhoods were made up of suburban homes on quarter-acre lots: our cities were rebuilt around the freeway, and to buy groceries, you had to do high-stress driving in high-speed traffic.

In the course of the twentieth century, the American middle-class moved from streetcar suburbs, where houses were on one-tenth acre lots and people walked, to sprawl suburbs, where houses were on one-quarter acre lots and people drove every time they left home. Yet the extra cost of sprawl did not made neighborhoods more livable. All the automobiles made neighborhoods noisier, more congested, and less safe for children then the streetcar suburbs had been. The nearby open land that attracted people to suburbia was paved over, replaced by more freeways, more strip malls, and more tract housing. The sense of community disappeared, as local shopping streets were replaced by anonymous regional shopping centers.

Traditional Neighborhood Design

Today, traditional neighborhoods are becoming popular again. The new urbanism, the most important movement in urban design today, is building neighborhoods that are like the streetcar suburbs and the urban neighborhoods of a century ago.

To promote walking and to conserve land, new urbanist suburbs are built at higher density than conventional suburbs – 8 or 10 units per acre instead of the 4 units per acre typical in post-war suburbia, a density that is high enough to support some shopping within walking distance of most homes. New urbanist suburbs also have narrow streets, in order to save land and to slow traffic.

New urbanist neighborhoods have a variety of land uses within walking distance of each other. There are some streets that have only housing, but there are also shopping streets within walking distance of the homes. Ideally, there should be transit stops on these shopping streets, also within walking distance of all the homes, though this is not always possible in today's developments.

New urbanist neighborhoods have a continuous street system, similar to the street grid of older cities and towns. Typical post-war suburbs have streets that are cul-de-sacs or are extremely curved, so even if you live near shopping, the trip there is so roundabout and long that it is difficult to walk. By contrast, the streets in new urbanist towns are direct enough that it is possible to walk to nearby shopping, as well as to drive there.

Finally, new urbanist neighborhoods have development that is oriented toward the sidewalk to make it more pleasant for people to walk. Shopping streets are designed like traditional Main Streets, with stores facing the sidewalk and housing or offices above. Off-street parking is behind the stores, so it does not interrupt the continuous store frontages facing the pedestrians on the sidewalk. On this sort of street, the stores bring business to each other: after shopping in one store, people will often walk up and down the street just to look at the other people and the store windows – very different from the suburban strip mall, where people drive from one store to another even when they are going to two stores on the same block.

Residential streets are also oriented toward the sidewalk. Homes have small front yards, and they have front porches and front doors facing the sidewalk to make them more welcoming to pedestrians. Garages are in the back, and in some cases, there are second units above the garages, to increase density further and to provide a variety of different types of housing for a diverse population.

This sort of street design works for automobile traffic, and it is far better for pedestrians than conventional suburban design. People get to know their neighbors, because they see them walking through the neighborhood to go shopping and see them at the local shopping street.

Because its best known projects are suburbs, there is a popular misconception that new urbanism just a different method of designing suburbs. Actually, it is a traditional approach to designing cities and towns as well as suburbs.

The new urbanists use the same principles of traditional urban design in urban neighborhoods that they use in suburbs. They build an old-fashioned continuous street grid, which works both for pedestrians and automobiles. They orient development to the sidewalk, to encourage people to walk among different uses. They do not let parking lots disrupt the pedestrian feel of the street.

But the greatest obstacle to this sort of traditional urban design is that, in most of America, it is illegal.

Developers who want to build new urbanist neighborhoods almost always must go through a burdensome process to get around zoning laws that require low-density, single-use suburban development. Most developers are not willing to spend the extra time and money needed to get zoning variances, so they build the conventional suburban development allowed by zoning.

The National Association of Governors has estimated that about one-third of Americans would prefer to live in traditional neighborhood developments, but that only 1 percent of the new housing available is in this type of neighborhood, because zoning laws all over the country require developers to build low-density, single-use suburbia. The Congress for the New Urbanism has estimated that, in a decade, because of demographic changes and continuing changes in taste, 55 percent of all American homebuyers would prefer to live in traditional neighborhoods, if they had the choice.[24]

Transforming American Cities

If we encouraged the development of walkable neighborhoods, instead of making it illegal, American cities could be transformed as dramatically in the next few decades as they were during the post-war decades. According to a recent study, two-thirds of the development that will exist in America in 2050 has not yet been built,[25] so we have a huge opportunity to transform our cities if we get this new development right.

It is important to transform our cities to reduce automobile dependency, because freeway-oriented sprawl neighborhoods are less livable than traditional walkable neighborhoods and because sprawl puts a great economic burden on Americans by requiring every adult to own a car. It is urgent to transform our cities to help deal with global warming.

Government should support public transportation and transit-oriented development as vigorously as it supported freeways and sprawl during the post-war decades, so we can build walkable, transit-oriented neighborhoods during the next few decades as quickly as we build sprawl during the 1950s and 1960s.

This new development is needed to give Americans the choice of living in walkable neighborhoods. After more than a half century of government support for sprawl, most Americans no longer have this choice. They have to live in auto-dependent neighborhoods, because that is where the overwhelming bulk of our housing is.

Demand for housing in walkable neighborhoods has increased dramatically because of demographic changes: less of the population is made up of families with children, who are most likely to want to live in suburbs. Because suburban zoning laws have prevented us from building enough housing to keep up with this demand, housing prices in walkable neighborhoods are much higher than in sprawl suburbs. Decades ago, urban housing was cheaper than suburban housing, but now urban housing in many metropolitan areas sells for 40 percent to 200 percent more per square foot than housing in sprawl suburbs. Walkable neighborhoods in the suburbs also command a big price premium: for example, an upscale apartment in downtown White Plains, NY, sells for about $750 per square foot, while an upscale house in a nearby sprawl suburb typically sells for $375 per square foot.[26] The large price premium shows that there is a shortage of walkable neighborhoods.

New pedestrian-oriented development would not only benefit people who want to live in those walkable neighborhoods. It would also benefit people who want to live in sprawl suburbs, by reducing the scarcity of housing in general. During the post-war decades, the boom in suburban housing did not just help people to live in the new suburbs; the overall supply of housing increased so much that it also held down housing costs in older urban neighborhoods. Since the 1970s, housing construction has slowed, and housing prices have gone up both in cities and in suburbs. For environmental reasons, the only way we can increase the supply of housing enough to make housing more affordable is by promoting public transportation and transit-oriented development.

Public Transportation

From the 1950s through the 1980s, almost all federal transportation funding was used to build freeways. Beginning in the 1990s, the federal government made some transportation funding flexible, so metropolitan areas could spend it on either freeways or public transportation. About

$129 billion of the funding for Federal Highway Administration programs between 1992 and 2002 was flexible funding, about 58 percent of the total funding. But of this flexible funding, the states spent only 5.6 percent on public transportation and the rest on highways.[27]

The federal government should make all of its transportation funding flexible, and the states should realize that the only way to solve their traffic problems is to build more public transportation and transit-oriented development rather than building new freeways.

In addition, the federal government should end the burdensome requirements that make it far easier for states to build highways than to build public transit. Currently, transit projects must be reviewed and approved individually before they get federal funding, while states can get funding to build highways without this onerous review and approval.

We will have to keep maintaining existing freeways, but spending to create new transportation capacity should not go to new or expanded freeways. It should go to public transportation and to pedestrian improvements.

Transit-Oriented Development

As we build more public transportation, we should also create incentives for developers to build walkable neighborhoods near transit stations. The federal government should come up with some financial mechanism to provide low-cost financing for housing in transit-oriented developments, which would stimulate the same sort of intense building around transit stations that the FHA stimulated around suburban freeways in the 1950s and 1960s.

There would have to be standards to determine whether development qualified for this financing. Development would have to be near a transit stop, connected with transit by a continuous street system, and so on. This development would not necessarily have to be extremely high density: around transit stations in the center city, we would build apartments, but around transit stations at the edge of the city, we could build the sort of streetcar suburbs that the new urbanists are now designing, with walkable street networks, with apartments above the shopping on Main Street, and with free-standing houses as the main housing type.

In addition to financial incentives, we need to change our zoning laws to promote transit-oriented development. Financial incentives can help get some transit-oriented development built, particularly new greenfield developments in undeveloped areas, but in areas that are already developed, local opposition is generally the greatest obstacle to new transit-oriented development. We can deal with this obstacle by shifting from conventional zoning laws to form-based codes.

Conventional zoning regulates density by setting limits such as maximum height, minimum setback, and maximum Floor Area Ratio (FAR) of new development. This conventional zoning allows many possible arrangements of the buildings, so it often leads to intense local controversies about the design of new buildings in existing neighborhoods. Neighbors want the new building to be set back in ways that move it further from their own homes, and they also want buildings to be smaller than the maximum height and FAR allowed by zoning. Neighbors can delay the approval process for years, a major obstacle to building infill housing that would make already developed areas more pedestrian and transit-oriented.

By contrast, form-based codes prescribe the form of the building. For example, rather than a minimum setback from the sidewalk, they have a build-to line, which might require the front of the building to be 10 feet or 15 feet from the sidewalk. Rather than a maximum FAR, they outline the building envelope.

If a good form-based code has been adopted, developments could be approved by right if they conform to the code and do not need variances. For example, the code should prescribe setbacks that protect the neighbors, so there should be no need for the Zoning Board to listen to protracted arguments from neighbors demanding larger setbacks.

There could be a tremendous surge of transit-oriented development, if the federal government provided financial incentives for building transit-oriented developments and if states required cities to adopt form-based codes for sites near transit, with approval by right for developments that conform to these codes.

A major push for public transportation and transit-oriented development could transform our cities in the next few decades. It could balance all the freeway-oriented neighborhoods built since the end of World War II with a new generation of walkable, transit-oriented neighborhoods. It could increase the housing supply, keeping housing affordable. It could reduce greenhouse gas emissions dramatically. And it could give Americans the option of saving money and living more simply by moving to neighborhoods where driving is an occasional convenience rather than an everyday necessity.

There is No Free Parking

To help transform American cities, we should also apply a key principle of a politics of simple living: people who live more simply should not be forced to subsidize people who are heavier consumers.

Today, everyone is forced to subsidize the automobile, whether or not they drive. For example, the costs of streets and traffic signals are paid for out of cities' general funds, so everyone pays for them through sales taxes and property taxes – including people who use only one-tenth as much street space because they bicycle or take public transportation rather than driving.

The most blatant subsidy to the automobile is "free" parking. Businesses generally provide free parking for their employees: 95 percent of all employees who drive to work park for free.[28] Virtually all new housing provides parking for residents at no extra cost. Most businesses provide free parking for customers.

The subsidies are large. It costs $7,000 to $15,000 for each space in a surface parking lot (depending on the cost of land), $20,000 to $30,000 for each space in a parking structure and $30,000 to $60,000 for each space of underground parking. Each person gets two spaces, one at home and one at work, plus more free parking at shopping centers, at parks, and at other services.

Free parking makes it much harder to build affordable housing. A small studio apartment might be only 500 square feet. A parking space takes up 300 to 350 square feet, including the space for driving within the parking lot as well as the parking space itself. Because many cities and suburbs require 1.5 spaces per unit, the area required for parking could be about as large as the total floor space of a small apartment. If the parking is structured or underground, it increases construction cost per housing unit dramatically; as a result, suburban apartments are likely to be built at low densities, so they can be surrounded by surface parking lots.

Of course, all this "free parking" is not actually free. Employers account for employee parking as part of the cost of labor, and they have to pay lower wages and salaries to make up for this extra cost. Likewise, developers have to charge higher prices for housing to pay for the parking they include, businesses have to charge higher prices to pay for the cost of the parking they provide, and everyone must pay these higher prices, whether or not they drive.

There are more equitable ways of dealing with the cost of parking.

Many environmentalists have called for laws requiring a "parking cash out" for employees. Instead of providing free parking, employers would charge a fee for parking that covers its full cost, and they would also give their employees a transportation allowance that is large enough to pay this parking fee. If employees drive to work alone, they can use the transportation allowance to pay the parking fee. If employees commute in two-person carpools, they can keep one half of the parking allowance for themselves. And if employees bicycle or walk to work, they can keep the entire parking allowance for themselves. It is estimated that this plan would cut commuter traffic by 15 to 25 percent, and it would give a substantial cash bonus to people who do not use the parking because they do not drive to work.

Likewise, we could require landlords, condo developers, and in some cases even single-family-housing developers to charge separately for the housing unit and for the parking. In denser cities where parking is structured, this could reduce the cost of housing dramatically for people who do not own cars.

Car-Free Housing

Some environmentalists have also called for changes in the zoning laws to allow car-free housing. New housing complexes would be built without parking, and people who live there would agree by contract not to have cars, though they could rent cars for occasional use. This would lower the price of housing, and the price would tend to stay low because there is less chance of gentrification if residents are not allowed to own cars. Car-free housing would work best in neighborhoods with residential permit parking: a number of cities allow on-street parking in some neighborhoods only for residents, who can get parking permits for their cars. People living in car-free housing would not be eligible to buy permits, so they could not cheat by owning cars and parking on the street.

Great Britain recently made it legal to build car-free housing, and the idea has been catching on in that country. The London Borough of Camden alone has approved construction of 3,500 car-free housing units, whose residents cannot have parking permits. Car-free housing has also been approved in Brighton, Bristol, Portsmouth, Edinburgh and Leeds.[29]

We could also create entire car-free neighborhoods by zoning areas with good transit service to require that all housing must be car-free housing. This housing would attract people who want to downshift economically and work part time, so these neighborhoods would be filled with people during the days. Residents would get to know their neighbors, because they would walk to local stores to do their shopping and walk to local parks with their children. And the neighbors would be interesting to know, because the people who live in these neighborhoods would have free time to pursue their own interests.

During the 1950s, old neighborhoods such as Greenwich Village in New York and North Beach in San Francisco, became popular for just these reasons: you could live there cheaply because they had old, low-cost housing and had shopping within walking distance, and they attracted interesting people because you could live there cheaply. But these neighborhoods were victims of their own success, and they became so popular that rents soared. Their success shows that there is demand for this sort of neighborhood: if cities began to zone for car-free neighborhoods in locations with good transit service, many people would want to live in these neighborhoods, at least during part of their lives. And these neighborhoods could be interesting enough to attract visitors and shoppers from the rest of the city, like the old Greenwich Village and North Beach.

The new neighborhood of Vauban, built on the site of a former army base that is a ten-minute bicycle ride from the center of Freiburg, Germany, is a car-free neighborhood designed specifically to attract families with children. Parking is available only at a garage at the edge of the neighborhood, and spaces sell for 17,500 euros each. There are four kindergartens, a Waldorf school and many playgrounds in this neighborhood, where one-third of the 4,700 residents are less than 18 years old. When kindergarten lets out, there are not lines of cars waiting to pick up the children; instead, there are long lines of parents on bicycles with trailers that carry children – a very convenient and low-stress way to get around your neighborhood, if it is a car-free neighborhood where you do not have to worry about being run down by traffic.[30]

There are many opportunities for similar development in the United States. For example, New York City is planning to rezone industrial land in Williamsburg and Greenpoint to allow high-density housing in a central location, and some of this could be a car-free neighborhood.

Currently, people who do not have their own cars still have to put up with the environmental costs of their neighbors' cars. Their neighborhoods are noisy, congested, and unsafe for children and bicyclists, because the streets are filled with cars. Car-free neighborhoods give people a real trade-off: if you opt to live in one of these neighborhoods, you lose the convenience of having a car, but you get the benefit of having a quiet neighborhood, pleasant public spaces, streets that are safe for your children, and stores that you can bicycle to without being crowded off the road by cars. If people had the opportunity to get the benefits of a car-free neighborhood in exchange for the inconvenience of not having a car, many would consider it a good trade-off – particularly if they could take advantage of the financial savings to cut down on their work hours and have more time to enjoy their car-free neighborhood.

Employee parking cash-out, car-free housing, and car-free neighborhoods are all meant to give people more choices. People still could still be auto-dependent if they chose, but they would also have these new options that they do not have today. In fairness, the people who choose to live without cars should not have to subsidize the people who choose to own cars.

Cities and Simpler Living

With traditional neighborhood design and alternative transportation, we could spend much less on housing and transportation and have cities that are more livable than our cities are today.

With a shift from freeway-oriented sprawl to transit and pedestrian-oriented neighborhoods, the cost of transportation could be cut roughly in half, because trip lengths would be cut dramatically and many trips would shift to walking and bicycling.

Likewise, with a shift from conventional sprawl suburbia to traditional neighborhood developments, the cost of housing could be cut by about 30 percent, according to the most extensive study of the subject.[31]

Overall, Americans could save about one-third of what they spend on housing and transportation if they chose to live in neighborhoods built like traditional streetcar suburbs, which are more livable than post-war suburban sprawl – and some people could save even more by choosing to live in car-free neighborhoods.

Chapter 4
Family Time and Child-Care Choice

Most Americans do not have enough time for their families. The average American child spends ten hours per week less with parents now than in 1970.[32]

We face this time famine because the economy takes up so much of our time. Fifty years ago, the typical family was supported by one parent working 40 hours a week. Today, the typical family is supported by two parents working 80 hours a week.

The issue of family time offers the best opportunity to convince most Americans that the hypergrowth economy has failed to improve our lives. Most people care enough about their children that they could see they would be better off consuming less and working less in order to have more time for their families.

Unfortunately, mainstream liberals generally do not focus on policies that would increase family time. Instead, they keep insisting on the same tired policies that liberals supported in the beginning of the twentieth century. The federal government should spend more money to provide universal preschool. The federal government should spend more money on schooling. The federal government should spend more money on after-school and summer programs. These policies take it for granted that parents do not have enough time for their children, so the children must constantly be in programs of one sort or another.

The demands for more spending on schooling made sense in 1900. At that time, only 6 percent of Americans graduated from high school, and urban elementary schools often had 50 children or more in a class. There was a real need for more funding for the school system.

These demands make no sense today. Spending on education has increased dramatically during the last century, and the evidence shows that we in the United States now spend more than enough on schooling. As we will see, international comparisons and historical comparisons show that we have moved far beyond the point where spending more on schooling improves education.

We do need to improve the quality of schools, but that is not primarily a matter of spending more money. And rather than spending more money on preschools, after-school programs, and other forms of child care, we should be looking for ways to let parents spend more time with their children.

Instead of Day Care

As a first step, we should end the current discrimination against families that care for their own children by giving child-care funding equally to all families with preschool children.

Currently, federal tax laws allow a tax credit of up to $1,050 per child for child-care expenses. This is one of the most widely used tax credits, totaling about $3.2 billion for child care and other dependent care.[33]

This income tax credit goes to families with children in day care, from the poorest to the wealthiest (though the credit is reduced from 35 percent to 20 percent for high-income families). Affluent dual-income families get a child-care tax credit, but families get nothing if they work shorter hours and sacrifice income so they can have time to care for their own children.

Instead, we should offer a tax credit to all low and middle-income families with preschool children, whether or not these children are in day care. The credit should be phased out for families with higher incomes: a dual-income family that earns $150,000 per year can afford to pay for its own child care.

The current tax credit gives people an incentive to work longer hours and spend less time with their children, because it pays for day care and gives nothing to families who work less and care for their own children. Most child-care proposals from liberals carry the same bias even further by proposing even bigger programs that give nothing to families who care for their own children.

If we simply leveled the playing field, we would give many families the opportunity to live more simply and have more family time.

Child Care and the Family Budget

The ideal child-care policy would be to give low and middle-income families with preschool children non-discriminatory tax credits that are large enough to pay the entire cost of day care, about $7,000 per year for each child. Families who need day care, such as single parents, could use this credit to pay for the day care. Most families could choose whether to use this credit to pay for day care or to help them work shorter hours and have more time to care for their own children.

Child-care advocates claim that we need more day care and preschool because the average family now needs two incomes to get by. This claim shows that they are totally blind to the failings of the growth economy. They apparently do not know that the average family earns two-and-a-half times as much today (after correcting for inflation) as in 1950, when most families cared for their own children.[34] They are blind to the greatest failing of our economy: families have trouble getting by despite their higher incomes because of all of the compulsory consumption that is forced on them.

Even if we ignore the possibility of reducing compulsory consumption (for example, by building walkable neighborhoods), we could give the average family the choice of caring for its own children just by giving the price of day care to the family directly, as a non-discriminatory tax credit.

The average woman's income after taxes is $18,998. One estimate calculates that the additional costs of the woman's working are $14,500, including $7,000 for day care. The net added income is $4,498. This estimate of the additional costs of working is an example, not a statistical average, but it is a reasonable estimate of what many families must pay in order to earn second incomes.[35]

If we had non-discriminatory child-care tax credit of $7,000 for each preschool child, the amount needed to pay for day care, the credit for one child would be greater than the net benefit of the second income. This credit alone would be enough to make it economically possible for families to work shorter hours and care for their own children. Of course, families with two preschool children would be even further ahead if they cared for their own children rather than putting them in day care.

In combination with work-time choice, this policy would let both men and women live more balanced lives, with time for both work and family.

Fifty years ago, the typical family was supported by a man working forty hours a week. If this were a reasonable world, the entry of women into the workforce would mean that the typical family today would be supported by two people working twenty hours a week, dividing the forty-hour week between them. Instead, the typical family today is supported by two people working eighty hours a week between them.

We have gotten so far out of balance, because we have inflexible work hours and because we have inflexible child-care policies that discriminate against people who care for their own children.

The Failure of Preschool

Child-care advocates often support their demands by claiming that preschools can improve children's academic performance, but they are distorting the evidence. In reality, the overwhelming majority of studies show that preschools can improve the academic achievement of poor, at-risk children to a small extent, but they have no effect at all on the achievement of middle-class children.

Here is one example of the usual distortions from mainstream liberals. Hillary Clinton writes:

> significant headway has been made in the field of biology, where researchers have begun to grasp how the brain develops. ... Dr. Frank Goodwin, former director of the National Institute of Mental Health, cites studies in which children who could be described as being 'at risk' for developmental problems were exposed at an early age to a stimulating environment. ... At the age of four months, half of the children were placed in a preschool with a very high ratio of adult staff to children. ... those in the experimental group averaged 17 points higher in IQ tests.[36]

Clinton exaggerates the program's benefits for at risk-children: IQ initially increases by 17 points, but the improvement diminishes over time, and by the time the children reach high school, it is less than 5 points, not enough to make a large difference in school achievement.[37]

Even more important, Clinton does not mention that the at-risk children in preschool did much worse than the national average, even though they did better academically than at-risk children who did not go to preschool. For example, 30 percent of the children in one of the most successful of these programs had to repeat a year in school, compared with 56 percent of the children who stayed home – an improvement over the at-risk children who stay at home, but still far worse than typical middle-class children.

It is not surprising that the benefits of these programs were small, since studies have shown that differences in quality of preschool account for only 1 percent to 4 percent in the differences in children's scores in tests of cognitive development, while the rest can be attributed to differences among their families.[38]

Constant repetition has convinced middle-class parents that their children's brains would be hard-wired to make them more intelligent if they were in preschool during the first three years of their lives, but in reality, the studies overwhelmingly show that preschool has no lasting benefit for middle-class children.

The reason is that preschools providing "a stimulating environment" for poor children just do what middle-class parents already do. Studies have shown that children are more successful in school if adults talk to them long before they have learned to speak, read to them, sing to them, give them interesting toys to play with, have repeated affectionate interactions with them. Most middle-class parents already do this, but many low-income parents do not talk or read to their infant children.

You do not need a degree in brain science to do these things, but some parents need to be told how important it is to do these things. We could improve child raising dramatically by funding a large-scale public education campaign with advertisements showing pictures of parents talking to infants and reading to toddlers, and giving information about how much this helps the children in later life.

Public health improved dramatically because of the anti-smoking campaigns of the 1970s and 1980s, which spread the word that people should do more to protect their own health. Education will improve dramatically when we spread the word that people should do more to educate their own preschool children.

More Money or More Time for Children

We need to ask the same question about older children that we are asking about preschool children: Should we spend more money schooling them, or more time raising them?

Mainstream liberals usually say that the federal government should spend more money on schools and on after-school and summer programs. Yet the figures show that we have reached a point where spending more money on schooling no longer improves educational achievement.

In the United States, per pupil spending on schooling today is more than 2.5 times what it was in 1963 (after correcting for inflation), but test results show that the students learn less. In 1950, American schools spent only $1,583 per student (in 2001-2002 dollars), a very small amount compared with the $8,259 per student that we spent in 2001-2002,[39] and at that time, increased spending was still needed. During the 1960s and 1970s, spending on education soared, and class size went down dramatically,[40] but scores on the SAT and other standardized tests plummeted. During the early 1980s, achievement began to improve again – and as it happens, this is just when spending on education stopped increasing for a few years because of Reagan's budget cutbacks, before it began to increase again during the late 1980s. Figure 4 shows very clearly that there is now no correlation at all between spending and achievement.

International comparisons of spending and achievement, shown in Figure 5, point to the same conclusion. For example, the United States spends far more on education than the average of the other industrial nations, but our results are worse than average: in the Third International Mathematics and Science Study, the most extensive international effort to test for academic achievement, American students had a score of 500 in Mathematics, while the other industrial nations had an average of 522. Other international tests of academic achievement have similar results: the United States scores either slightly below average or far below average. We spend over 50 percent more on schooling than the average of the other industrial nations, but we have lower achievement than the average of the other industrial nations.

Many studies have shown the same thing, beginning with the large-scale statistical studies by James Coleman in the 1960s and Christopher Jencks in the 1970s, which showed that quality of schooling has a very small influence on educational achievement compared with quality of family and community life.[43]

The demands for more money for schooling are useless, and the demands for more money for after-school and summer programs are a real threat to our children's development, because they are leading us toward a society where children's activities are controlled during so much of their time that they have little time left to do anything serious on their own.

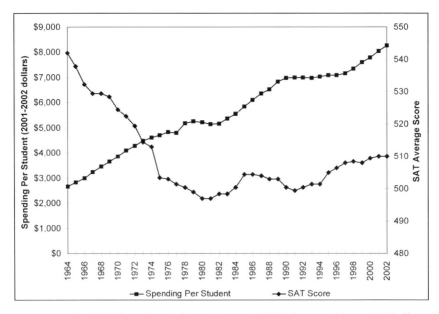

Figure 4: US Educational Spending and SAT Scores Since 1960s[41]

To grow up into autonomous adults, children and teenagers need time for their own thoughts and their own projects. For example, people who grow up to be serious readers virtually all begin by reading for pleasure on their own time – even though they may have disliked the books they had to read for their school assignments.

Not very long ago, playing baseball with the other kids on the block was an essential part of American childhood. As the children chose teams and argued about disputed plays, they learned to organize themselves and to make decisions on their own.

Not very long ago, American children and teenagers had plenty of free time for play, reading, and solitude, during the hours after school and during their long summer vacations. But today, most parents want to put their children in after-school and summer programs, because there is no one to take care of them at home. They put their children on teams where the adults organize their baseball games, rather than letting the children learn to form teams and organize games themselves.

If parents had more free time, they could be home to casually watch over children who are alone in their rooms or playing with the other kids on the block – as parents typically did fifty years ago. Today's parents should at least have this option: they should not feel that they are forced to put their children in after-school programs and full-time summer programs

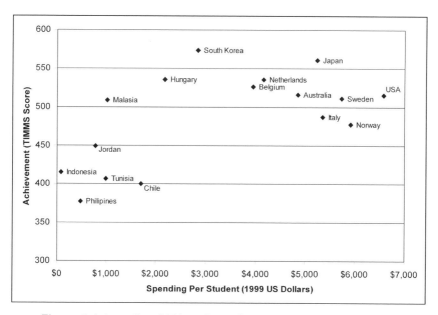

Figure 5: International Educational Spending and Achievement[42]

because it is impossible for them to be home when their children come back after school, and their children would be latchkey children coming home to an empty house.

Activities or Commodities

When we step back and look at them in perspective, the conventional liberal idea that we should provide universal free preschool does not seem very different from the conventional idea that we should provide universal free parking.

Both violate the key principle of a politics of simple living: people who consume less and do more for themselves should not have to subsidize people who consume more. Both violate this principle because they subsidize only the consumers: people who walk or bicycle do not get any benefit from free parking, and people who care for their own toddlers do not get any benefit from free preschools, but everyone has to pay higher prices or higher taxes to support the free parking and free preschools, whether or not they use them.

We subsidize parking and child-care because we consider them necessities. Most families cannot buy their groceries without finding a parking space, and most families cannot survive economically without putting their children in day-care and earning two incomes.

Yet there was a time when most Americans got along perfectly well without either of these "necessities." One hundred years ago, Americans did not need all this transportation because they usually got around on their own power by walking. Fifty years ago, Americans did not need all this child care because they usually took care of their own preschool children.

As Ivan Illich said, the modern economy tends to convert activities into commodities. Activities that most people used to do themselves – getting around and caring for children – have become commodities that the economy produces for people to consume – transportation and child care.[44]

People who demand universal free child-care (like people who cannot imagine the world without free parking) are so completely mystified by the modern economy that they cannot conceive of the possibility that people could break out of their consumer dependency and begin to do more for themselves again. Their demands overlook the real needs of most Americans, who would be better off if they consumed less transportation and spent more time walking, and who would be better off if they consumed less child care and spent more time with their children.

Chapter 5
Optimism About the Future

During the early and mid-twentieth century, there was a widespread faith that technology and economic growth would bring us a better future. Liberals appealed to the majority of Americans by promising to give everyone a share of this affluent future.

Now, liberals need to develop a vision of a better future that suits our time as well as the old vision of economic growth and affluence suited the 1950s.

Today, we are no longer optimistic about the future. We can see that, because of global warming, looming energy shortages, and other environmental problems, economic growth might make the world a much worse place before the end of this century. And we have lived with affluence long enough to know that it is not all that it promised to be: for example, the average American drives twice as much today as in the 1960s, and we can see that spending all this time on the freeways does not make our lives better but does spread ugliness across the landscape. The freeways were an important part of the "affluent society" of the 1950s, but now they look more like a blight than like a benefit.

Today, we can see that the 1950s vision of endless consumerism will give us a flood of products that does not make our lives significantly better but that does make our planet significantly less livable.

As an alternative to this bleak view of the future, this book is sketching a vision of a better future that we can have after the age of hypergrowth. This future must have three elements.

First, as we have seen in earlier chapters, we must allow people to downshift economically, so they can take the benefit of increased economic efficiency in the form of more free time for their families and their own interests, rather than in the form of more consumer goods of dubious human value. Giving people this choice would slow growth, taking the edge off of the world's environmental crisis.

Second, to appeal to the majority of Americans, we have to give everyone a chance to share in this future of economic comfort and abundant leisure, just as liberals in the early twentieth century wanted to give everyone a chance to share in the benefits of economic growth and affluence. Today, many Americans cannot imagine cutting back on their work hours, because inequality has increased so greatly that low income Americans are no better off than they were forty years ago.

Third, we need to deal directly with ecological problems such as global warming, depletion of topsoil, and the toxic chemicals in our environment. These are familiar problems that many environmental groups have addressed.

These three things could bring us a future where we all have a comfortable middle-class standard of living, where we have a stable global environment, and where we have enough free time to realize our humanity fully. Instead of a bleak future of empty consumerism and ecological crisis, we could have a future where we have moved from the realm of necessity to the realm of freedom – a future where, for the first time in history, most people have been freed from the need to spend most of their time just earning a living and instead can focus on living well.

Taxes and Equality

Historically, liberals supported progressive taxes to reduce inequality. Today, as we reach the limits of economic growth, we need to return to this historical liberal position: if we want everyone to live comfortably, we need to give everyone a fair share of what the economy can produce sustainably.

Under a progressive income tax system, there are higher tax rates on higher incomes: for example, everyone might pay no tax on the first $10,000 of income per person, pay a low tax on the second $10,000 of income, and keep paying higher taxes on higher increments of income. The justification for progressive taxation is that low income people need all of their income for necessities such as food and housing. As people's incomes get higher and higher, they spend a larger and larger portion of it on luxuries. If we made everyone pay the same tax rate, taxes would cause much more hardship among the poor, who would sacrifice necessities to pay their taxes, than among the rich, who would sacrifice luxuries to pay their taxes.

During the depression, the Roosevelt administration created a very progressive income tax system, with a maximum tax rate of 91 percent on income above $2 or $3 million a year in today's dollars. This was a time of economic hardship, when there was an obvious need to give moderate income people a decent share of the nation's wealth.

During the 1960s, liberals began to abandon their earlier support for progressive taxation. This was a time of rapid economic growth, when it was tempting to avoid the political conflicts caused by redistributing income and instead rely on growth to help raise everyone's income. The motto of the time was "a rising tide lifts all boats," the saying that John F. Kennedy used to defend his tax cuts against criticisms that they would primarily benefit the rich.

Kennedy lowered the maximum tax rate to 70 percent. He claimed that, because he eliminated loopholes for the rich that had been added to the tax system during the 1950s, the government could raise more revenue with this lower rate, but he also claimed that lower rates for the rich would stimulate economic growth, and he created a tax credit for investments in new plants and equipment in order to promote growth.

Kennedy's tax cuts helped cause the economic boom of the 1960s, and together with Lyndon Johnson's large deficits, they helped cause the inflation of the late 1960s. During the 1970s, the inflation already built into the economy compounded with higher prices of oil and other natural resources to bring a combination of double-digit inflation and economic stagnation – the so-called "stagflation" of the 1970s.

During the 1980s, Ronald Reagan said he would cure these problems with supply-side economics. Claiming that lowering taxes would stimulate economic growth, Reagan cut the maximum income tax rate to 27 percent, down from Kennedy's 70 percent. Republicans since Reagan have continued to lower taxes on the rich: today, one of their pet proposal is to end the estate tax, a tax cut that would only benefit millionaires.

Reagan supported lower and less progressive taxation by claiming that the new tax structure would bring faster economic growth and that the benefits of growth would "trickle down" to everyone – just as Kennedy had claimed that "a rising tide lifts all boats."

Today, it should be clear that the benefits have not trickled down. The benefits of prosperity were widely shared before 1970, but typical Americans have not gotten a fair share since then.

Figure 6 compares median household income, which is the income that 50 percent of all households earn less than, with mean household income, which is the average that we get by adding all household incomes and dividing by the number of households. The median indicates how well the typical middle-income household is doing, while the mean can be pulled up by a small minority of very rich households. We can see the difference

41

if we imagine a group of 100 people, with 99 earning $50,000 per year and with 1 earning $100,000,000 per year. The median income for this group is $50,000, which shows how well the typical middle-income person in the group is doing. The mean income is over $1,000,000, but that high mean does not show that the typical middle-income person is rich; it just shows that one person in the group is super-rich and pulls up the average.

In Figure 6, we can see that median and mean income grew at about the same rate during the 1950s and early 1960s, when prosperity was shared across all income levels. During the late 1960s, mean income began to grow a bit more quickly than the median income, and the gap has widened ever since, as inequality has increased and the very rich have gotten a bigger and bigger piece of the pie. If inequality had not increased, median income would have gone up as rapidly as mean income, and median income would be about 20 percent greater than it is today, so typical middle-income people would be better off than they are today.

The graph also shows that growth of income did not accelerate because of Reagan's tax cuts. On the contrary, the growth rate was highest during the 1950s and 1960s, when we had a very progressive tax structure. (Growth of income was also very high during the dot-com boom of the late 1990s, but some of the gain was lost during the dot-com bust of the early 2000s.)

Today, we need to reject the rising-tide and trickle-down theories of wealth creation, because it is environmentally destructive to promote faster

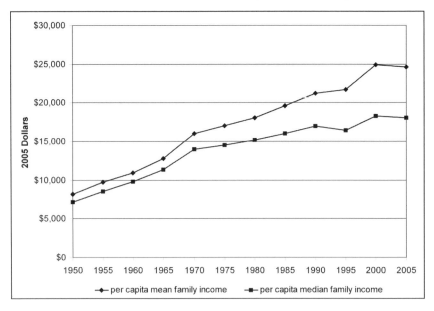

Figure 6: Per Capita Median and Mean Household Incomes[45]

economic growth as a substitute for progressive taxation. As we reach the environmental limits of growth, we need to reject tax policies aimed at creating a hypergrowth economy in favor of policies that give everyone a fair share of what we can produce sustainably. A more progressive income tax and greater equality should become key items of the liberal agenda once again.

Since the "Reagan revolution" of the 1980s, conservatives have distracted the public's attention from their plans to transfer wealth from the middle class to the very rich by focusing on culture wars, claiming that "elitist" liberals want to destroy our traditional family values. Liberals seem to have cooperated in making the culture wars a central political issue by ignoring increased economic inequality, and we would do much better politically by focusing on this bread-and-butter economic issue again.

Liberals should emphasize how much inequality has increased since the Reagan revolution. In 1981, the United States ranked thirteenth among 22 developed nations in income inequality. Today we rank last, the most unequal country in the developed world.[46]

The top 10% of Americans now make 48.5% of all income, almost as much as the remaining 90% of Americans. And the top one-tenth of 1 percent of American make as much income as the bottom 50 percent of Americans; in other words, the wealthiest 300,000 Americans now make as much income as the bottom 150,000,000 Americans.[47]

Inequality is caused partly by larger economic trends – globalization has eliminated most of the well-paying factory jobs that unskilled American workers could get decades ago – but changes in our tax system have made inequality much worse than it needs to be and much worse than it is in other industrial nations.

We can reduce inequality dramatically by returning to a more progressive income tax system, similar to the system we had before the 1980s – not by increasing taxes but by changing tax rates so the very rich pay their fair share and the middle class pays less. In addition, we should expand the Earned Income Tax Credit for low and moderate income working people, so everyone who works earns a living wage.

This approach would be an obvious win for liberals. For decades, conservatives have won elections by calling for tax cuts and accusing liberals of wanting to increase taxes – without mentioning that their cuts were designed to benefit the very rich. Liberals could obviously appeal to the majority of Americans by saying that they do not want to increase taxes but want to shift taxes from the middle class to the rich, so the rich pay their fair share again, as they did before the Reagan revolution.

Whenever anyone talks about making the rich pay their fair share of taxes, the Republicans accuse them of class war, but there is an obvious answer to this: there is already a class war in America, it has been going on since the beginning of the Reagan presidency, and it is a war against the great majority of Americans on behalf of the wealthiest 5 or 10 percent of Americans.

A Carbon Tax Shift

To create a sustainable economy, we must deal with a wide range of environmental problems, but we will not discuss all these problems here because mainstream environmental groups have already discussed them at great length. We will just look at how a carbon tax shift could deal with our biggest environmental problem, global warming, and at the same time, help reduce inequality by making our tax system more progressive.

The two most prominent proposals for controlling global warming are:

- **A Carbon Tax:** Fuels would be taxed based on how much carbon dioxide they emit, with the tax increasing every year. Though it is a called a carbon tax, it should also tax other greenhouse gases, such as methane.

- **A Cap-and-Trade System:** Government would set an upper limit on the amount of carbon dioxide (and other greenhouse gases) that industries can emit, with the limit decreasing every year. Businesses that reduce emissions below their limit could sell emission rights to businesses that remain above their limit.

Economists tell us that a carbon tax would be the most efficient way to control global warming, but the conventional wisdom is that it is not politically feasible to create a major new tax, so cap-and-trade is our only realistic alternative.

Yet a carbon tax could be politically feasible if it were presented not as an added tax but as a tax shift meant to lower other taxes, such as the income tax, by shifting the tax burden to polluters.

One carbon tax bill introduced in congress would tax carbon dioxide at $10 a ton the first year and would raise the tax by $10 a ton each year until carbon dioxide emissions are reduced to 80 percent less than their 1990 level. There is obviously very little support for this sort of open-ended tax increase, but if we made it a carbon tax shift instead of a carbon tax, it would be just as effective in combating global warming but would be far more feasible politically. We would simply have to add the following provision to the carbon tax:

> Each year, the Internal Revenue Service will return all the money collected by the carbon tax to taxpayers as a refundable income tax credit, given equally to each taxpayer.

This sort of carbon tax shift would have tremendous advantages over keeping our current income tax and adding a cap-and-trade system to control carbon dioxide emissions.

Income tax has no benefit except raising revenue. A carbon tax has this benefit of raising revenue, and it has the additional benefit of dealing with our most pressing environmental problem, global warming. If a carbon tax and an income tax both raised the same amount of revenue, the carbon tax would provide much more overall benefit.

A carbon tax could apply to imports, while a cap-and-trade system could only apply to domestic products. Products imported from other countries could be required to declare how much carbon dioxide is generated in producing them and transporting them to America, and they would have to pay the carbon tax on these emissions. Thus, a carbon tax would help convince other countries to reduce emissions, in addition to reducing American emissions. It would also favor locally produced goods over imported goods, because local goods use less energy for transportation. Reducing the distances that goods are transported is important to controlling climate change in a global economy: a single nation can help deal with the issue of global transportation by adopting a carbon tax shift, but a single nation's cap-and-trade would not affect transportation outside that nation.

A carbon tax would encourage technological innovation. Currently, for example, photovoltaic solar power is much more expensive than power generated by burning coal, but there are several new technologies being developed that have the potential of cutting its cost dramatically, such as thin-film solar panels and improved manufacturing techniques. A carbon tax that increases each year would give businesses a powerful incentive to invest in the research and development needed to develop better solar technologies and other forms of clean energy. This tax would harness the market to innovate in the directions where innovations are most needed.

A carbon tax shift would be progressive. As a general rule, the more you consume, the more carbon dioxide you emit – both directly and because of the energy embodied in the products you buy. Thus, a carbon tax shift would take more revenue from wealthier people who consume more, and it would return this revenue as a tax credit given equally to everyone.

A carbon tax shift would let us charge enough to be effective. To reduce emissions 80 percent by 2050, as we must do to avoid the worst effects of global warming, we probably need a tax that begins at $20 per ton of carbon dioxide – which is only one cent per pound of carbon dioxide – and that increases by 10 percent a year. There is no chance of passing a tax increase this large, but it could be possible to pass a carbon tax shift that does not involve a net tax increase.

The conventional wisdom says that only cap-and-trade is politically feasible, but we could change what is politically feasible by emphasizing that cap-and-trade means that money generated by the system goes to businesses, while a carbon tax shift means that the money goes equally to every taxpayer. We should also emphasize that, with this sort of a plan, the majority of Americans would not pay any income tax: after a decade or two, only the very rich would still pay income tax, and most Americans would get a check back from the IRS instead of paying taxes.

There would be some short-term economic sacrifice with any plan to reduce carbon emissions, because cheap and dirty energy from coal and other fossil fuels would be replaced by more expensive clean energy at first. Initially, we will have to pay extra for energy, but we will be better off because we avoid the global warming caused by dirty energy. After a time, new technologies should bring down the cost of clean energy.

The short-term issue is what happens to the money used as an incentive to convince people to shift to clean energy. With a carbon tax shift, that money would go back to all taxpayers equally to help them pay the higher energy prices.

To emphasize that this is not a tax increase, we should always call it a "carbon tax shift" instead of a "carbon tax." In fact, a bill proposing this plan would probably be very successful if it were named "The Global Warming Reduction and Income Tax Reduction Bill."

Two Possible Futures

This book has looked at policies that could offer us an optimistic vision of the future: give people the choice of downshifting economically, so they can consume less and have more free time, tax carbon dioxide and other forms of pollution, so we can harness the market's power of innovation to provide us with clean technologies, make the income tax more progressive, so everyone has a share of this better future.

Currently, mainstream politicians are only talking about technological fixes for global warming, such as cleaner energy technologies. There is no talk among politicians – conservative or liberal – about more fundamental changes that would slow economic growth by giving people the option of working less and spending less in order to have more free time. The unspoken assumption is that growth should continue at its current rate endlessly, meaning that consumerism would continue to become more and more excessive.

We can see that this technological fix is not good enough by comparing two possible futures, one that continues consumerism and growth as usual, and one that moves toward simpler living. We will look at the two extreme possibilities, so we can see clearly the decision that we face, though the actual future may well be somewhere between these two extremes.

Growth As Usual

If we continue promoting economic growth, we will continue to run up against the two main ecological constraints that our economy faces today: global warming and limits to our supplies of energy and other natural resources.

Global warming has already begun. Unless we act dramatically to slow global warming, it will cause flooding, desertification, famine, and more human suffering than anything that has ever occurred in the past.

Limited energy supplies are already pushing up gasoline prices. Geophysicists predict that world oil production will peak some time in the next decade or two, and the scarcity will drive prices up far higher than they are now.

Though gasoline price increases get the most publicity, there have also been price increases for a wide range of natural resources. Between the end of 1999 and the end of 2007, oil prices increased by 268 percent. During the same period, corn prices increased by 150 percent, soybean prices increased by 176 percent, nickel prices increased by 242 percent, natural gas prices increased by 259 percent, wheat prices increased by 269 percent and copper prices increased by 289 percent.[48] Economists are beginning to say that there has been a fundamental shift in world markets, as increased demand from China and other developing nations causes demand for natural resources to press against the limits of supplies.

We are trying to respond to the twin problems of global warming and tight resource supplies purely by using technological solutions. One popular fix is biofuels, such as alcohol produced from crops, which could provide liquid fuels to substitute for gasoline. But the land used to grow biofuels is no longer available to grow crops. Even if we used cellulosic ethanol from switchgrass, the most efficient source of bio-fuels currently being discussed, replacing all of American gasoline consumption would take about 700 million acres, more than 70 percent of the land now used for farming in America.[49] We can get a large amount of energy from agricultural wastes and from energy crops grown on marginal land, but nowhere near what we need to support our current level of gasoline use.

Widespread use of biofuels could lead to widespread world hunger, since Americans can spend more to feed their cars than people in developing nations can spend to feed their children. In fact, the use of corn to produce ethanol has already driven up world food prices: for example, the price of tortillas in Mexico doubled in 2006, causing hardship for 50 million poor people who rely on tortillas as their main food source.

Other sources of clean energy are more benign: solar energy uses much less land than biofuels, but there is no immediate way to use solar electricity as a liquid fuel to substitute for gasoline and jet fuel, and if our energy consumption keeps growing at its historic rate, even solar energy would use about one-third of America's land by the end of this century.

Even if we do come up with an abundant source of clean energy, endless economic growth will strain the supplies of other resources. Ecological Footprint studies by William Rees and Mathis Wackernagel show that, if everyone in the world had the same standard of living as Americans, it would take five earths to provide the resources they would consume. It is possible to develop technologies that use resources more efficiently, but if growth continues at its recent rate, it will become more and more difficult to avoid overshooting the earth's carrying capacity.

If we continue on the path of endless hypergrowth, we will be running a constant race against the problems caused by growth – and we will need endless crash programs to develop technologies to provide more energy, to provide more raw materials, and to manage ecological breakdown. No matter how much technological progress we make, it will be hard to keep up, as economic growth would tend to increase pollution and demand for resources endlessly. The faster the rate of economic growth, the more likely it is that we will lose this race and that there will be economic collapse and die-back – like the collapse and die-back that happened on Easter Island after it was deforested, but on a world-wide scale.

If we continue promoting consumerism and hypergrowth, as we have since the end of World War II, it is likely that global warming and rising resource prices will prevent most of the world from emerging from poverty. We can expect wars for resources, and we can expect famine in Africa and parts of Asia, with pockets of uneasy affluence remaining in the United States, Europe, and parts of Asia, where people still drive SUVs around their neighborhoods.

These problems have already begun. We are fighting a war in Iraq to secure our energy supplies. The hunger and genocide in Darfur are caused partly by global warming, as UN Secretary-General Ban Ki-moon recently pointed out: before the drought in east Africa, black farmers welcomed Arab herdsmen to their lands, where they shared the wells, and fighting between these two groups broke out only when there was not enough food and water for all because of desertification caused by global warming.

The second row of Figure 7 projects recent growth of Gross World Product into the future. It shows the key fact that, as long as people do not have the option of working shorter hours and using increased productivity to increase their free time, rapid growth must continue endlessly, purely to avoid unemployment, even after per capita GWP is $4 million or $11 million per year – just as rapid growth is now considered necessary in the United States, purely to avoid unemployment, whether or not people want more products. Those levels of per capita GWP could not be sustainable, and at some point, they would lead to ecological collapse.

Simpler Living

As an alternative to this consumerist future, imagine that we adopt the sort of policies discussed in this book and, to strengthen the contrast, imagine that people take full advantage of these policies to live more simply.

We could be economically comfortable and have a middle-class standard of living, with adequate education, health care, and housing. We would avoid the excesses of consumerism that Americans have come to take for granted during recent decades – for example, people would not drive gas-guzzling SUVs, and they would not live in neighborhoods where they have to drive every time they leave their homes – but this sort of consumerism adds very little to the sum total of our happiness. Even apart from environmental concerns, we would be better off spending less money on things we do not need and having more time to do the things we really want to do.

Simpler living in the United States and the other developed nations would take some of the edge off of the crisis of global warming and energy

	1950	2000	2050	2100	2150	2200	2250	2300	2350
Comfort	2,582	7,392	16,420	16,420	16,420	16,420	16,420	16,420	16,420
Growth	2,582	7,392	21,162	60,586	173,451	496,574	1,421,643	4,070,017	11,652,041

Figure 7: Per Capita GWP in the Two Futures (2000 dollars)[50]

shortages. If the world adopted strict limits on carbon dioxide emissions and the developed nations moved away from consumerism, we could limit world temperature increases and avoid the worst effects of global warming, such as extreme weather events.

The developing nations could continue to grow until they reached this same level of economic comfort. At that point, world economic growth would end because needs would be satiated. People would have the economic goods that they need and want, and they would stop demanding more once they had enough. Here, we are still bringing the contrast between these two futures into sharp relief by imagining that the people of the world not only adopt the sorts of policies recommended in this book but also take full advantage of them by avoiding consumerism.

The first row of Figure 7 projects recent growth of per capita GWP, assuming that growth ends when per capita GWP reaches the same level as the United States' per capita GNP in 1965, a time when America was prosperous enough to call itself "the affluent society." This could be enough to provide everyone in the world with a comfortable middle-class standard of living, and it could be ecologically sustainable.[51] The world could emerge from poverty during the twenty-first century, as the developed nations emerged from poverty during the twentieth century.

Early in the twentieth century, many economists believed that economic growth would end in this way: as we moved beyond scarcity and reached the point where we had enough, people would want to have more leisure rather than having more to consume.

In his 1930 essay "Economic Possibilities for our Grandchildren," the great economist John Maynard Keynes predicted that, one hundred years in the future, the economy would reach the point where we would have the leisure needed to live well.

All through recorded history, Keynes said, there were economic ups and downs, but there was not any general trend toward increased production and greater prosperity: "From the earliest times of which we have record – back, say, to two thousand years before Christ – down to the beginning of the eighteenth century, there was no very great change in the standard of life of the average man living in the civilized centers of the earth."

But during recent centuries, there has been continuing economic progress, because new technologies have made production more efficient, and because capital accumulating at compound interest has been invested in those technologies.

Now, Keynes said, "mankind is solving its economic problem." In the past, "the economic problem, the struggle for subsistence, always has been

... the primary, most pressing problem of the human race – not only of the human race but of the whole biological kingdom from the beginnings of life." But in the future, "a point may soon be reached, much sooner perhaps than we are all aware of, when these needs are satisfied in the sense that we prefer to devote our further energies to non-economic purposes."

When that time comes, he concluded, "man will be faced with his real, his permanent problem – how to use his freedom from pressing economic cares, how to occupy the leisure which science and compound interest will have won for him, to live wisely and agreeably and well."[52]

The Choice We Face

Keynes' prediction of more leisure made sense in 1930: writing at a time when work hours had been getting shorter since the beginning of the industrial revolution, Keynes naturally expected more of the same. But things look different today: the work week stopped decreasing after Keynes wrote, because the postwar economy deliberately promoted consumerism to provide everyone with 40-hour-a-week jobs, and because most people do not even have the option of working less.

Today, we can see a future of increased leisure is not inevitable, as Keynes thought. There are two possible futures: we can continue to promote consumerism and rapid economic growth to provide everyone with 40-hour a week jobs, or we can move away from consumerism and toward shorter work hours. We have to make a deliberate choice between those two futures, and the sort of world that we will have during the coming centuries depends on the choice we make now.

If we continue our current long work hours and hypergrowth, we are headed toward a future of natural resource shortages, toward a future where global warming will probably continue even if we reduce carbon dioxide emissions from each unit of output, toward a future where there will be famine and massive movements of global-warming refugees across the world, toward a future where extreme weather will make the earth less livable.

If we live more simply and also reduce carbon dioxide emissions from each unit of output, we could be headed toward a future where our biggest economic problem will be the one that Keynes foresaw: that the economy has reached a point where people work short hours to produce that things they need and want, so they have the "problem" of using their free time to live wisely, and agreeably, and well.

To make the contrast clear, we have looked at two extreme alternatives, a future where long work hours, consumerism and hypergrowth continue indefinitely, and a future where growth stops when people are economically comfortable. As a practical matter, of course, the future may be somewhere between the two: even if we give people the option of downshifting, some people, maybe most people, will continue to be more or less consumerist.

But today, we are forced into the extreme alternative of hypergrowth – using all our productivity gains for more growth and more consumerism – because most Americans do not even have the option of working shorter hours – using some productivity gains for more free time. We should at least offer that option to people who think it would make their lives more satisfying or think that they have an obligation to live more lightly.

During this century, as people see how much damage consumerism is causing, there could be a powerful movement toward simpler living. If this movement becomes widespread, it could be significantly easier to control global warming and other ecological problems. But this movement will not spread if people do not have even have the option of working less and consuming less.

Chapter 6
From Old Left to Green

America faces two key economic realities today that we did not face a century ago: growth has created a surplus economy so that most Americans consume more than they need to live comfortably, and growth has become an urgent threat to the global environment.

Policies to let us downshift economically could have been appealing to many Americans for the past several decades. Most Americans are short of time and are burdened by an expensive standard of living, so some people could be attracted by policies that give them the option of downshifting and having more time for their families and their own interests.

Now that we know we have entered the age of global warming, these policies are not only appealing but are also essential. The world's environment cannot support the excesses of the consumer economy.

Yet mainstream liberals have not begun to advocate the policies that we need to deal with today's surplus economy. Instead, they repeat the same policies that the left backed a century ago to deal with the problems of a scarcity economy, focusing on demands that government spend more money to provide people with more services.

Liberals no longer have the compelling vision that they had in the mid-twentieth century, because these old-left policies are marginal in today's America. These policies focus on the problems of the minority who do not have enough, and they ignore the problems of the majority. This does not mean that we should abandon our attempts to deal with the problem of poverty, but it does mean that we should stop ignoring the new problems of affluence.

The Decline of the Left

The world has changed since Eugene V. Debs first ran as the Socialist Party candidate for president in 1900.

In 1900, average American income was near what we now define as the poverty level, and large-scale industrialism was increasing production dramatically. Socialists wanted the government to use the productive capacity of modern industry to benefit working people, rather than just the rich. They believed the government should control the means of production and manage them for the benefit of the masses. As part of this economic planning, they believed the government should set up centralized organizations, on the industrial model, to provide the masses with basic necessities, such as housing, health care, and education.

New Deal and Great Society liberals had the same bias but were more moderate. They believed that the government should stimulate economic growth in the private economy to provide jobs and generate wealth – and it should take a large share of this wealth in the form of taxes that it would use to provide working people with housing, health care, education, and social services.

Today, the average American's income is more than five times what it was in 1900. A minority of Americans still do not have adequate housing, education, or healthcare, and we still need to help that minority. But the central political challenge of our time is to let the affluent majority live simpler and more satisfying lives.

During the first half of the twentieth century, liberals had a vision of the future that appealed to the majority of Americans – the vision that modern technology could bring abundance for everyone. If the government harnessed the modern economy to benefit everyone, then the working class could have decent education, decent health care, and decent housing for the first time in history.

This was the vision of liberals during the 1930s, when poverty was still the nation's central economic problem. New Deal liberalism was based on the idea that the federal government should promote the growth of the private economy, should build public works such as dams, highways, and power projects to complement the growth of the private sector, and should take advantage of this prosperity to fund programs that provide everyone with decent housing, education, and jobs.

But this vision began to lose its appeal during the post-war decades, when America shifted from a scarcity economy to an affluent economy. Post-war affluence gave most middle-class Americans decent housing and education, so you could no longer appeal to the average American by promising to provide these things. The freeways and power projects built by the federal government began to look less like symbols of a better future and more like symbols of an ugly consumer economy.

Rather than developing new policies to deal with the new problems of affluence, the left marginalized itself during the 1960s and in the decades that followed by focusing on the problems of underprivileged minorities – on groups that do not get a big enough share of the economic pie.

During the 1960s, many leftists began to say that the working class, which had always been the left's main constituency in the past, was no longer part of the left's coalition, because the workers had moved to suburbia and started thinking of themselves as middle-class. At that point, the left turned away from the working-class majority that had always been their mainstay and instead began to appeal to minorities.

But there are two problems in appealing to minorities. First, if you focus on helping minorities and ignore the problems of the majority, it is hard to win elections. Second, if you focus on bringing minorities into the affluent mainstream, you are focusing on a mopping-up operation and not on the central problems of the economy as a whole.

During the 1970s, the left tried to expand its appeal by reaching out to new minorities, such as the disabled, and by redefining large groups of people as minorities, such as women. With women redefined as an oppressed minority, the majority of Americans were minorities. But it is not good enough to say that a dozen oppressed groups should all get a bigger piece of the economic pie and to ignore the fact that the pie is becoming less and less nourishing.

Back in the days when people believed the modern technological economy was bringing us a better future, liberals could appeal to Americans by promising to give everyone a share of that prosperous future. But by the 1970s, there were widespread doubts that technology and economic growth were bringing us a better future.

And liberals, with a tragic failure of vision, did not develop a new ideal for the future that makes sense in the context of our new surplus economy.

Instead, American liberalism split into two factions during the 1970s. On one hand, the old left still dominated liberal thinking about social policy, endlessly repeating the left's traditional idea that we should spend more money to provide services – more money for child care, more money for education, more money for affordable housing, more money for health care, and more money to provide jobs – policies that had been central in a scarcity economy but that were marginal in an affluent economy. On the other hand, the environmental movement dominated liberal thinking about technology – but it focused on how much damage the technological economy does to the natural environment, and it did not develop new social policies that would help people to take advantage of the affluent economy to live well.

This failure of mainstream environmentalists to develop social policy is obvious if we ask: What is the environmentalist policy on child care? This is an issue that could make the majority of Americans understand that our hypergrowth economy has failed to give us a better life, since keeping up with the consumerist standard of living has made it impossible for most people to take care of their own preschool children, as almost all Americans did a few generations ago. If we campaigned for policies that give Americans child-care allowances and flexible work hours, we could rein in the growth economy by encouraging parents to work less and consume less so they can care for their own children. But environmentalists have not thought about this social issue at all, because they focus on the physical environment. As a result, liberals still repeat the old-left mantra that we should provide more funding for child care – without considering that the child care is needed so people can work the long hours that fuel hypergrowth.

The failure of mainstream environmentalists to develop social policy is even more obvious if we ask: What is the environmentalist policy on providing jobs? Virtually no one in the political arena is supporting choice of work hours,[53] though this is the only social policy that would let us slow economic growth without increasing unemployment, and at the same time would let us live more satisfying lives. Environmentalists sometimes claim that investing in sustainable technologies would create more jobs, showing that they do not think at all about the real social change that we need – a change to a less consumerist, less workaholic society, to a society where we can work shorter hours rather than feeling compelled to create more jobs.

Since the 1960s, liberals have passed laws against racism and sexism, an important social advance. But liberals still have not dealt with the most destructive "ism" of the twenty-first century – consumerism.

A Convenient Truth

Unlike mainstream environmentalists, some radical environmentalists do talk about simpler living, but their prescriptions are usually so harsh that they could never be politically successful.

For example, a recent article agonizes over dozens of cases where environmentalists use paper napkins, use plastic bags for the fruit they buy at the farmer's market, and so on, and then it finally advances this ideal example of an environmentalist who really lives the changes that we need:

she ... began to live on the land in a tent. She farms six acres without tillage or chemicals of any kind. ... She built a rough house by raiding dumpsters for building supplies and trading labor with friends. ... What attracted me to her talk was its title: "Creating a Farm and Homestead on Marginal Land (While Penniless)." [She] was the most inspiring person I'd seen in a long time.[54]

Needless to say, most people in the world are not going to be very inspired by this idea of doing long hours of hard labor to scrape out a subsistence living – particular not people in the developing nations, who are trying to escape from just this sort of harsh, impoverished life.

The idea that simpler living means more drudgery is the biggest obstacle that prevents environmentalists from developing a vision of a better future. Environmentalists' fascination with the clothes line is one obvious example. Typically, the *New York Times* featured the story of a woman who said she was following "energy-saving tips from Al Gore, who says that when you have time, you should use a clothesline to dry your clothes instead of the dryer." When she tried it, "I briefly gave up – the dryer was so much easier – but then tried again." She finally got in the habit of doing all this extra work, but she found that her electric bill was "still too high, so we're about to try fluorescent bulbs."[55]

Doing your laundry with a tub and washboard and then hanging it out to dry was one of the most hated of women's traditional tasks: women usually did it on Monday, and the work was so hard that they called the day "blue Monday." Do environmentalists really believe that this sort of thing can attract wide public support? If so, maybe they should tell people to get rid of their clothes washers as well as their dryers, and bring back the washboard as well as the clothes line, so they can spend every Monday doing laundry all day.

If we promote forms of energy conservation that involve increased drudgery, then people will start associating energy conservation with drudgery. They are likely to decide that conserving energy is so burdensome that they will support nuclear power or strip mining to avoid it.

Mainstream environmentalists advocate conserving energy by using technological fixes, such as fluorescent light bulbs, which do not change our way of life at all.

Environmentalists should go a step further by advocating for simpler living that changes our way of life for the better – not for clotheslines and more drudgery but for changes that reduce the amount of drudging work we must do.

Environmentalists should be saying that the consumerism of the past few decades has made us work harder but generally has not improved our lives. The organization named Redefining Progress has created a Genuine

Progress Indicator, which corrects the Gross Domestic Product by subtracting environmental costs of growth and what economists call "defensive expenditures," extra spending on health care, education, commuting, and urbanization that is necessary only to deal with the costs of growth. They found that America's per capita GDP has risen steadily during the last sixty years, but that our actual economic well being rose until the early 1970s and then began to decline.

For example, as we have seen, the average American drives twice as much now as in the 1960s, because we have built so much urban sprawl. There is no real benefit to spending all this extra time on the freeways, but there is the real economic burden of paying for the extra driving, there is real environmental damage caused by the carbon dioxide emissions from the automobiles, and there is a war in Iraq to secure the gasoline supplies. On balance, we are worse off because of all this extra driving. Most city planners have realized this fact, so new urbanists now are designing walkable neighborhoods like the streetcar suburbs of a century ago – and most people can see that these walkable neighborhoods are better places to live than sprawl suburbs, even if we disregard larger environmental issues.

New urbanist neighborhoods are a model for a politics of simple living that could attract widespread public support. These neighborhoods have become popular because they are more attractive, more comfortable, and more convenient than sprawl suburbs, though they involve consuming less land and less gasoline.

The politics of simple living outlined in this book applies a similar idea across the entire economy. Many people would find their lives easier and more pleasant if they had the option of downshifting economically by working shorter hours and consuming less, if they had the option of living in walkable neighborhoods rather than in sprawl suburbs, and if they had the option of taking care of their own children rather than consuming child-care. Our lives could be much easier: as economist Dan Aronson says, this is the "convenient truth" that could help us deal with the inconvenient truth of global warming.

This book is an attempt to develop some of the policies that are needed. It is not complete, but it does show the direction we should be moving. It is the opposite direction from the conventional idea that we need more growth purely to create jobs, but it is also the opposite direction from the idea that we should conserve energy by hanging out our laundry on the line. It is the opposite of both of these, because it involves less drudgery, not more – less work producing things we do not really want to have so we have more time to do things we really want to do.

The policies sketched out in this book would cause major changes in our society and economy. Business would probably fight against these policies, just as business fought during the 1930s against a shorter work week and for a "new gospel of consumption."

The difference is that, during the 1930s, no one saw the dangers of economic growth, but today we see that growth can bring more problems than benefits. There are predictions that world petroleum production will peak within a decade. There is a consensus among scientists that global warming will cause massive famine and displacement unless we act dramatically to slow greenhouse-gas emissions. These looming problems provide a powerful argument for simpler living.

Cynics object to the politics of simple living by saying that people will never change and will always want to consume more. There is no historical basis for this claim. Pre-industrial peoples do not have this attitude toward consumption: early European imperialists in Africa were disappointed to find that the people there would only work long enough to earn the money that they needed and then would quit.

The vicious circle of more consumption and more work is a product of the industrial revolution, which brought the world into the age of economic growth for the first time, and this vicious circle was institutionalized in our post-war economic policies. Now, we face environmental crises that demand a change as profound as the change brought by the industrial revolution, a move beyond the age of hypergrowth.

The only question is how much damage we do before we decide to change. There will probably have to be a crisis before these sorts of policies are implemented. This crisis may come sooner than we think.

Now is the time for us to develop and advocate the policies that will be needed when the crisis of growth comes. As we move into the age of resource scarcity and global warming, we must develop a new politics of simple living.

Notes

[1] U.S. Bureau of the Census, *Statistical Abstract of the United States: 2006* (Washington, DC, 2006) p. 448.

[2] Source: 1900-1957: Susan B. Carter et al., editors, *Historical Statistics of the United States: Earliest Times to the Present* (New York, Cambridge University Press, 2006) p. 3-463; 1958-2000: George Thomas Kurian, ed, *Datapedia of the United States: American History in Numbers*, third edition (Lanham MD, Bernan Press, 2004) p. 134.

[3] John de Graaf, David Wann, Thomas H. Naylor, *Affluenza: The All-Consuming Epidemic* (San Francisco, BerrettKoehler, 2002) p. 130.

[4] Source: 1840-1890: *Historical Statistics*, p. 2-301; 1890-1925: *Historical Statistics*, p. 2-303; 1930-1995: *Historical Statistics*, p. 2-306 to 2-307; 2000: *Statistical Abstract 2006*, p 414.

[5] Benjamin Kline Hunnicutt, *Work Without End: Abandoning Shorter Hours for the Right to Work* (Philadelphia, Temple University Press, 1988) p. 82.

[6] Vance Packard, *The Waste Makers* (New York, David McKay, 1960) p. 17.

[7] Cited in de Graaf et al., *Affluenza*, p. 42.

[8] Juliet B. Schor, *The Overworked American: The Unexpected Decline of Leisure* (New York, Basic Books, 1991) p. 128.

[9] Schor, *Overworked American*, p. 133.

[10] Center for the New American Dream, www.newdream.org/live/time/timepoll.php.

[11] Source: *Statistical Abstract 2006*, p. 399. The 17% who work part-time because full-time work is not available combines the *Statistical Abstract's* categories: Slack work or business conditions, Could only find part-time work, and Seasonal work. This calculation omits the *Statistical Abstract's* categories: Vacation or personal day, Holiday, Weather related curtailment, and Job started during the week, since these are not actually part-time workers, though they worked less than full-time during the week surveyed.

[12] In 2005, the average American worker worked 1,804 hours in the year, while the average Dutch worker worked 1,367 hours in the year, less than 76 percent as much. Organization for Economic Cooperation and Development, *OECD Employment Outlook*, (OECD, Paris, 2006).

[13] Rudd Lubbers, "The Dutch Way," *New Perspectives Quarterly*, Fall, 1997, p. 15.

[14] David Rosnick and Mark Weisbrot, "Are Shorter Work Hours Good for the Environment?" Center for Economic and Policy Research (CEPR), 2006.

[15] In 1970, the average new house was about 1500 square feet. In 2005, the average new house was 2,500 square feet, according to the National Association of Home Builders. Fred A. Bernstein, "Are McMansions Going Out of Style?" *New York Times*, October 2, 2005.

[16] Schor, *Overworked American*, p. 107.

[17] During his confirmation hearings, Wilson was asked if he could make a decision as Secretary of Defense that conflicted with the interests of General Motors. He answered that he could not conceive of such a conflict happening "because for years I thought what was good for the country was good for General Motors and vice versa." This statement was widely quoted in the slightly modified form, "What's good for General Motors is good for the country."

[18] A national highway system was first proposed after a 1938 study by the Bureau of Public Roads led to a "Master Plan for Free Highway Development" that called for a 27,000 mile network of inter-regional highways, which would be limited access, would be elevated or depressed in urban areas, and would include inner and outer belt roads in City Centers to allow traffic to bypass central business districts. The 1952 and 1954 Federal Aid Highway Acts allocated $25 million and $175 million to build these roads, but this funding came out of general funds, and the acts were criticized for contributing to the federal budget deficit. The Federal Highway Act of 1956 increased the proposed length of the system to 41,000 miles and renamed it the National System of Interstate and Defense Highways. The Highway Revenue Act of 1956 created the Highway Trust Fund to pay the federal share of the cost of these roads and credited all revenue from the federal gasoline tax and other motor vehicle taxes to this fund. Today, the length of the Interstate Highway System has been increased to 45,024 miles.

[19] Martin Anderson, *The Federal Bulldozer* (Cambridge, Mass., MIT Press, 1964) p. 75.

[20] This was first suggested by Yacov Zahavi of the U.S. Department of Transportation. See Yacov Zahavi, *Travel Over Time*, Report PL-79-004 (FHWA, U.S. Department of Transportation, 1979). Yacov Zahavi and Antti Talvitie, "Regularities in Travel Time and Money Expenditures," *Transportation Research Record 750* (TRB, National Research Council, Washington, D.C. 1980) pp. 13-19. Yacov Zahavi and J. M. Ryan, "Stability of Travel Components Over Time," *Transportation Research Record 750* (TRB, National Research Council, Washington, D.C., 1980) pp. 19-26. A follow-up study showed that the time that Americans spend commuting to work has remained constant since the 1840s, when the move to the suburbs began as a reaction against the industrial revolution. J. M. McLynn and Spielberg, "Procedures for Demand Forecasting Subject to Household Budget Constraints" in *Directions to Improve Travel Demand Forecasting: Conference Summary and White Papers*, HHP-22 (Washington DC, Federal Highway Administration, 1978) pp. 115-197. Another follow-up study showed that the total amount of time that Americans budget to transportation tends to average about 1.1 hours per day, regardless of speed. J. M. Ryan and B. D. Spear, "Directions toward the Better Understanding of Transportation and Urban Structure," in *ibid.*, pp. 199-247. A later study updated Zahavi's analysis using data through 1990 and concluded that he was right to say that people have a constant time budget that they devote to traveling: Gary Barnes and Gary Davis, *Land Use and Travel Choices in the Twin Cities, 1958–1990*. Report No. 6 in the series *Transportation and Regional Growth* (Minneapolis: Center for Transportation Studies, 2001).

[21] Mark Hansen and Yuanlin Huang, "Road Supply and Traffic in Californian Urban Areas," *Transportation Research A*, Volume 31, No 3, 1997, pp. 205-218.

[22] Source: Vehicle miles traveled from *Historical Statistics*, p. 4-835 to 4-836 and *Statistical Abstract 2006*, p. 715. Population from *Historical Statistics*, p.1-26.

[23] See Sam B. Warner, Jr., *Streetcar Suburbs: The Process of Growth in Boston, 1870-1900* (Cambridge, Mass., Harvard University Press and the MIT Press, 1962).

[24] Congress for the New Urbanism, *The Coming Demand*, based on research by Dowell Myers, Elizabeth Gearin, Tridib Bannerjee, and Ajay Garde, University of Southern

California School of Policy, Planning and Development (San Francisco, Congress for the New Urbanism, undated).

[25] Reid Ewing, Keith Bartholemew, Steve Winkelman, Jerry Waters, and Don Chen, *Growing Cooler: The Evidence on Urban Development and Climate Change* (Washington, DC, Urban Land Institute, 2007) p. 18.

[26] Christopher B. Leinberger, "The Next Slum?" *Atlantic Monthly*, March 2008.

[27] No author named, "Flexing To Transit: Are State Leaders as Flexible on Transit as Federal Law?" *Surface Transportation Policy Project Progress*, vol. 12, number 2, October 2002.

[28] No author named, "New Report on Parking Cash-Out Law," *Institute of Transportation Studies Review*, (Berkeley, CA, Institute of Transportation Studies, July 2002).

[29] No author named, "The fond farewells to four wheels: New, car-free developments are catching on fast," *The Telegraph,* March 25, 2006. Car-free housing was allowed by the recently adopted section 106 of the national planning code.

[30] Isabelle de Pommereau, "New German Community Models Car-Free Living," *Christian Science Monitor*, December 20, 2006.

[31] This study, by Patrick Condon is included in the proceedings of the Alternative Development Standards Symposium, published by the Landscape Architecture Program of the University of British Columbia, Vancouver, British Columbia.

[32] During the 1970s and 1980s, white children lost 10 hours a week of parental time, while black children lost 12 hours. Sylvia Ann Hewlett and Cornel West, *The War Against Parents* (Boston, Houghton Mifflin, 1998) p. 48.

[33] Elaine Magg, "The Disappearing Child-Care Credit," Urban Institute, October 2007. This study points out that the child-care credit may become unavailable to upper-income families as an unintended side-effect of the alternative minimum tax.

[34] See Figure 6.

[35] Based on Jerome Segal, *Graceful Simplicity: Toward a Philosophy and Politics of Simple Living* (New York, Henry Holt, 1999) p. 66. Segal estimates that the second job requires the following additional expenses each year: day care, $7,000; second car $2,500; additional cost of lunches, $1,000; additional cost of food at home, assuming that the family eats one additional restaurant or take-out meal a week, $1,000; cost of a house cleaner one day a week, $2,500, additional cost of clothes for work, $5000; total additional cost: $14,500.

[36] Hillary Clinton, *It Takes a Village: And Other Lessons Children Teach Us* (New York, Simon & Schuster: Touchstone Books, 1996) pp. 56 - 61.

[37] John T. Bruer, *The Myth of the First Three Years : A New Understanding of Early Brain Development and Lifelong Learning* (New York, Free Press, 1999), p. 171. This book is the best account of how child-care advocates have misinterpreted brain science.

[38] Bruer, *Myth of the First Three Years*, p. 191.

[39] U.S. Department of Education, *Digest of Education Statistics 2004* (Washington, DC, National Center for Education Statistics, 2004) Table 163. The numbers represent total expenditure per pupil in average daily attendance in 1919-1920, 1949-1950, and 2001-2002.

[40] The pupil-teacher ratio in public and private elementary schools was 29.4 in 1960 and was 20.1 in 1980. The ratio has declined more slowly since 1980: in 1995, it was 18.7. *Digest of Education Statistics 1996*, p. 74.

[41] Sources: Figures on per pupil expenditure, *Digest of Education Statistics 2004*, Table 163; SAT scores, *Digest of Education Statistics 2004*, Table 129. These figures

apply to academic years: for example, the figure on the graph for 1964 actually applies to the academic year 1963-1964.

[42] Source: Achievement scores from National Center for Education Statistics (U.S. Department of Education and Institute of Education Sciences), *Highlights From the Trends in International Mathematics and Science Study (TIMMS): 2003*, published December 2004, p. 76. The values used in the graph are an average of the mathematics and science scores. Figures on spending from Unesco Institute for Statistics, *Financing Education - Investments and Returns 2002*, Table 9: Expenditure on educational institution per student (1999). The graph only includes countries that are available in both of these studies.

[43] The famous Coleman Report concluded that "When these [socio-economic] factors are statistically controlled, however, it appears that differences between schools account for only a small fraction of differences in pupil achievement." James Coleman et al., *Equality of Educational Opportunity* (Washington, DC, U.S. Government Printing Office, 1966) pp. 21-22. Christopher Jencks' massive study on inequality concluded that "qualitative differences between schools had relatively little effect on students' test scores ... differences between schools also had relatively little effect on students' eventual educational attainment." Christopher Jencks et al, *Inequality: A Reassessment of the Effect of Family and Schooling in America* (New York and London, Basic Books, 1972) p. 39. It also concluded that "We have shown that the most important determinant of educational attainment is family background.... Except for family background, the most important determinant of educational attainment is probably cognitive skill...." (pp. 158-159).

[44] Illich makes this point in many places. For example, Illich says, "Schools operate by the slogan 'education!' while ordinary language asks what children 'learn.' The functional shift from verb to noun highlights the corresponding impoverishment of the social imagination. ... Not only what men do but also what men want is designated by a noun. 'Housing' designates a commodity rather than an activity." Ivan Illich, *Tools for Conviviality* (New York, Harper & Row, 1973) p. 96-97.

[45] Source: Mean and median family income through 1995: *Historical Statistics*, p. 2-653. These Bureau of Labor Statistic based figures from *Historical Statistics* are supplemented with BLS figures for 2000 and 2005. Corrected using the Bureau of Labor Statistics Consumer Price Index from *Historical Statistics*, p. 3-159 plus later BLS consumer price indexes. Converted to per capita household income using average household size from U.S. Census Bureau, *Statistical Abstract of the United States: 2003*, p. 19, Table No. HS-12, plus later census bureau figures for household size.

[46] De Graaf et al., *Affluenza*, p. 78.

[47] David Cay Johnston, "Income Gap Is Widening, Data Shows," *New York Times*, March 29, 2007, pp. C1 and C10.

[48] Clifford Krauss, "Commodities' Relentless Surge: Chinese and U.S. Demand Push Food and Minerals Steeply Higher," *New York Times*, January 15, 2008, p. C1.

[49] No author named, "Bio-Hope, Bio-Hype," *Sierra Magazine*, September/October 2007, p. 50. Other biofuels would be much worse: replacing just 5% of American gasoline consumption with soybean biodiesel would take 138 million acres, about the size of Arizona and Colorado combined, replacing 5% with corn ethanol would take 117 million acres, about the size of Oregon and Idaho combined, replacing 5% with sugarcane ethanol would take about 41 million acres, about the size of Wisconsin, replacing 5% with cellulosic ethanol made from switchgrass would take about 35 million acres, about the size of New York.

[50] Source for Gross World Product, 1950-2000: Lester Brown et al., *World Watch Institute, Vital Signs 2002* (New York, WW Norton & Co., 2002) p. 59. Source for world population (divided into GWP to get per capita GWP): United Nations Population Division,

Department for Economic and Social Information and Policy Analysis, "World Population Growth From Year 0 To Stabilization." The "Growth" projection assumes that per capita GWP continues to increase indefinitely at the same rate as it increased between 1950 and 2000. The "Comfort" projection assumes that GWP increases at this rate until growth ends when per capita GWP reaches the same level as the United States per capita GNP in 1965.

[51] According to Mathis Wackernagel's studies of ecological footprints, it would take about five earths to maintain the world's current population of 6 billion at the United States' current level of consumption (see www.footprintnetwork.org). Assuming we use current technology, that means it would take 3.75 earths to maintain the world's projected peak population of 9 billion at the United States' 1965 level of consumption, which is about one half the United States' current level of consumption. Weizsacker and Lovins and have argued convincingly that we can increase resource efficiency four-fold over its current level by using cutting-edge technologies that are already available. Ernst Ulrich von Weizsacker, Amory Lovins, L. Hunter Lovins, *Factor Four: Doubling Wealth, Halving Resource Use* (London, Earthscan, 1997). Thus it should be possible to maintain the world's peak population at the standard of living of the United States in 1965 using current technology, if we shift rapidly to these more efficient and more sustainable technologies.

[52] All quotations in this section are from John Maynard Keynes, "Economic Possibilities for our Grandchildren," in *Essays in Persuasion* (New York, Harcourt, Brace & Co., 1932) pp. 358-373.

[53] Take Back Your Time is the one national group that actively supports the idea of making it easier for Americans to work part-time, but they have not yet had an impact on mainstream national politics.

[54] Janisse Ray "Altar Call for True Believers: Are we being change, or are we just talking about change?" *Orion* magazine, September/October 2007.

[55] Kathleen A. Hughes, "To Fight Global Warming, Some Hang a Clothesline," *New York Times*, April 12, 2007.